SOKA EDUCATION

For the Happiness of the Individual

DAISAKU IKEDA

Published by Middleway Press
A division of the SGI-USA
606 Wilshire Blvd., Santa Monica, CA 90401

© 2010 Soka Gakkai

ISBN 978-0-9779245-5-4

All rights reserved
Printed in the United States of America

22 21 20 19 18   4 5 6 7 8

Cover and interior design by Lightbourne

Library of Congress Cataloging-in-Publication Data

Ikeda, Daisaku.
  Soka education : for the happiness of the individual / Daisaku Ikeda. -- Rev. ed.
     p. cm.
  Includes bibliographical references and index.
  1. Ikeda, Daisaku. 2. Soka Gakkai. 3. Education--Philosophy. I. Title.
  LB880.I36.A3S66 2010
  370.1--dc22   2010030529

CONTENTS

Foreword by Victor Kazanjian   v
Dean of Religious and Spiritual Life, Wellesley College

Preface   xi

Introduction: John Dewey and   1
Tsunesaburo Makiguchi: Confluences of
Thought and Action (June 2001)

PART ONE: Addresses and Proposals   33

1. The Challenge of Global Empowerment: Education for a Sustainable Future (2002)   35
2. Reviving Education (January 29, 2001)   49
3. Serving the Essential Needs of Education (September 29, 2000)   75
4. Education Toward Global Citizenship (June 13, 1996)   109
5. An Outspoken Advocate of Educational Reform (June 4, 1996)   123
6. Teachers of My Childhood (2004)   135
7. The Teacher's Art (1998)   149
8. An Unforgettable Teacher (1998)   155
9. Humanity in Education (August 24, 1984)   161
10. Perspective on Virtue (January 26, 1992)   177
11. A True Restoration of Humanity (April 9, 1973)   189
12. The Fight To Live a Creative Life (April 18, 1974)   203

PART TWO: Brief Thoughts   211

Endnotes   225
Included Works   233
Index   235

FOREWORD

A new educational movement has been growing to renew the integral role of education in creating a healthy and peaceful world. Like independent streams winding their way down from different mountain peaks, the strands of this movement have emerged in different places and in different cultural contexts around the world. Recently, these streams have begun to merge and form a river, a single global movement that holds the promise for a renewed vision of the role of education in empowering individuals and shaping societies. One important tributary of this movement is the work of Daisaku Ikeda as he tells the story of the Soka educational movement in Japan and interprets its wisdom for the world.

My own work is based in a small liberal arts college in the northeastern part of the United States (Wellesley College) and has focused on exploring ways in which colleges and universities might better provide an educational experience in which students gain a deeper understanding of themselves, of others and of the world, and apply this learning as engaged global citizens. For a number of years I have been a part of a movement within the United States to examine the ways in which education falls short of these ideals. Our hope has been, as our member Parker Palmer writes in *To Know as We Are Known*, to "revision education…[in a way that] would result in a deeply ethical education, an education that would help students develop the capacity for connectedness that is at the heart of an ethical life."

It was in this context that in 1998 I first came in contact with the writings of Daisaku Ikeda in the text of a speech titled "A Matter of Heart" given at Peking University in 1990:

> It is people who will pave the way toward the future of our world, and there is no greater influence in the development of an individual than that of solid, human-centered education. Learning is the fundamental force that builds society and shapes an age. It nurtures and tempers the infinite potential latent in all of us, and it directs our energies toward the creation of values.

When I first read these words, I knew immediately that this man, whose words so poetically express the aspirations of all who believe in education as a transformational process, represents one of the essential streams of thought that feeds the river of educational reform. Since that time I have found Mr. Ikeda's writings to be a source of great wisdom that challenges people throughout the world to examine the values that form the foundation of their actions. Once again in this collection of Mr. Ikeda's writings, we are treated to a compelling and inspiring series of teachings on the principles of and possibilities for education.

By examining the particular story of the historic and contemporary movement to reform education in Japan, Mr. Ikeda provides teachings that will enrich the work of educators everywhere. His discourses on such topics as the pursuit of justice and human values in education, on creativity in education, and on education for global citizenship speak to the key philosophical and practical discourses that are taking place among educators on every continent. Drawing from the writings of philosophers and poets of all ages and places, Mr. Ikeda breathes new life into the ancient vision of education as the primary force for human liberation by applying these teachings to a contemporary context.

In his essay "Serving the Essential Needs of Education" (see p. 75), Mr. Ikeda points to the crisis in contemporary education that must be addressed if education is to reclaim its inheritance of this ancient vision: "The education system has therefore been reduced to a mere mechanism that serves nationalistic objectives, be they political, military, economic or ideological." The purpose of education is an essential question in considering the role of education in creating peaceful and just societies. For Mr. Ikeda this purpose must reflect the highest ideals of education. Ideals such as: "The wisdom to perceive the interconnectedness of all life and living. The courage not to fear or deny difference; but to respect and strive to understand people of different cultures and to grow from encounters with them. The compassion to maintain an imaginative empathy that reaches beyond one's immediate surroundings and extends to those suffering in distant places" (see "Education Toward Global Citizenship," p. 109).

Another aspect of Mr. Ikeda's teachings offered in this volume is the presentation of a Buddhist perspective on education based on these principles of wisdom, courage and compassion, a perspective he learned from the teachings of Soka Gakkai's first president, Tsunesaburo Makiguchi.

For those who do not yet know the groundbreaking work of Makiguchi on value-creating pedagogy, Mr. Ikeda paints a vivid picture of the life and work of this great Japanese educational reformer. Reviewing Makiguchi's life as well as offering an in-depth analysis of his philosophy of education, Mr. Ikeda brings the teachings of this great reformer to the world.

In November 2000, on behalf of The Education as Transformation Project in the United States, I had the honor of presenting Mr. Ikeda with the inaugural Education as Transformation award. This award is given to leaders from community-based, educational and religious organizations who are working to create a more peaceful and just world through a commitment to transforming the educational process to reflect a more holistic vision of learning. In such learning, spirituality and the pursuit of pluralism are seen as essential to fostering global learning communities and responsible global citizens.

The inscription on the award reads: "As president of Soka Gakkai International, Daisaku Ikeda has, throughout his lifetime, sought to root out and address the fundamental causes of human conflict and suffering and to promote the values of peace and respect for all people through education. Inspired by Soka Gakkai's founder, Tsunesaburo Makiguchi, and his disciple, Josei Toda, President Ikeda has advanced the philosophy of value-creation through his commitment to the areas of peace, culture and education. By founding an educational system that nurtures people of wisdom and humanity, President Ikeda and Soka Gakkai International offer a vision of an educational process, which by transforming the individual transforms the world."

If we are to transform our educational systems to be more responsive to the challenges that the world is presenting to the human community, we must listen to the wisdom of teachers from across the world, teachers such as Daisaku Ikeda. Only in this way can we implement the global movement for educational reform in our own local contexts.

—Victor H. Kazanjian Jr.
Dean of Religious and Spiritual Life and co-director of the Peace and Justice Studies Program at Wellesley College; co-founder and senior advisor to The Education as Transformation Project based at Wellesley College

PREFACE

What is the fundamental purpose of education?

Tsunesaburo Makiguchi, the father of Soka, or value-creating, education asserted that it is the student's "realization of happiness."[1]

Education exists for youth, who are the future. Education should encourage youth to realize their precious potential and to display their unique individuality with enthusiasm and vigor. Furthermore, education should teach youth to uphold the sanctity of life—for both self and others—so that they may create supreme value in their own lives as well as for society. These were Makiguchi's educational ideals.

Educators earnestly seeking their students' happiness will naturally come to treat them with unconditional trust and warm respect, instead of giving them instruction from on high. As Ralph Waldo Emerson writes: "The secret of education lies in respecting the pupil."[2]

One of the greatest problems in modern education, I believe, lies in its tendency to lose sight of students' happiness as its fundamental purpose.

Born in 1871, Makiguchi was a compassionate and loving educator who spent many years as an elementary school teacher and later became a school principal. He had many original and creative ideas in his specialty, geography. He also served as the founding president of the Soka Gakkai, an association that melded his educational theories with the philosophy of Buddhism he encountered late in life.

During World War II, Makiguchi directly opposed the Japanese military government for its infringement upon religious freedom. As a result, he was imprisoned and died at age seventy-three, a martyr to his unwavering convictions.

Makiguchi developed his value-creating educational theories based on his practical classroom experience. These theories took flight when coupled with his in-depth study and devoted practice of the Buddhist philosophy of Nichiren, who lived in thirteenth-century Japan.

Nichiren elucidated the inherent dignity of life shared by all people. He adamantly believed that humanity as a whole can transcend all differences and attain an unshakeable state of happiness.

Nichiren's belief was revolutionary in that it challenged the state power of feudal Japan built upon a rigid status system as well as the Buddhist establishment allied with the government. For this reason, Nichiren was continuously persecuted throughout his life.

Encountering similar persecutions, Makiguchi breathed new life into Nichiren's basic tenet of respecting all life. Even though the military government oppressed Makiguchi and caused his death in prison, it could not destroy his spirit. It was carried on by his disciple Josei Toda who later became the second president of the Soka Gakkai.

Toda, a superb educator in his own right, put Makiguchi's educational theories into practice, establishing a private school and fostering many talented individuals. One of his students was Dr. Hajime Yamashita, Japan's leading scholar of German literature. Reminiscing about his time spent under Toda's tutelage, Dr. Yamashita once said: "Mr. Toda burned with passion, an earnest and serious passion whose intense heat I could almost feel."

Though imprisoned with Makiguchi, Toda survived his teacher and was released from prison. What he began alone, in the aftermath of war, was the education of the masses— through his passionate dialogue with one person at a time. He knew all too well that such life-to-life communication was the only way to prevent war and build the firm foundation for peace.

As one of the students fostered and educated personally by Mr. Toda, I learned much from him in many fields of study. He entrusted me with the task of building an educational institution to put the ideals of Soka education into practice. The Soka educational system, from kindergarten through university level, was established out of my desire as a disciple to realize the noble dream for education shared by Makiguchi and Toda.

Makiguchi never set foot outside Japan, so his theories were formulated in the context of the Japanese educational system of his time. Yet there is a universality and timelessness to his ideas. As Dr. Dayle M. Bethel wrote in his work *Makiguchi, The Value Creator*: "In the study of the works of such prophetic educators as Makiguchi, the contemporary educator can gain valuable insights and understandings that will assist him in his efforts to provide effective educational experience for children and young people who are and will be participants in a postindustrial, global community."[3]

Not only was Makiguchi an excellent educator, but he was a great global citizen who was far ahead of his time. Playing a part in realizing Makiguchi's educational philosophy on the practical level, I have had many opportunities to speak with students and share in their experiences—both pleasant and unpleasant. Through many years of such talks with students, I have accumulated some insights into education and its challenges for the future and have occasionally delivered speeches on these topics.

This book is a collection of such addresses, including one I delivered at Teacher's College, Columbia University (see p. 109). My hope is for this book to be a source of encouragement and a helpful reference not only to educators but to students and parents as well.

In May 2001 the new campus of Soka University of America was dedicated in a picturesque setting in Orange County, California. I have said that I will devote what remains of my life to the cause of education, and I have acted true to this resolve. Education is my mission as a successor to the ideals of Makiguchi and Toda. Furthermore, I believe that humanity's peace and prosperity for the coming centuries can be built only upon the foundation of education. Now that we have entered the twenty-first century, I am resolved to work ever more earnestly and diligently for education.

In closing, I give my deepest appreciation to the editorial staff of Middleway Press for compiling and editing this book, thereby helping make the ideals of Soka education accessible to the English-speaking world.

INTRODUCTION

John Dewey and
Tsunesaburo Makiguchi:
Confluences of
Thought and Action

June 2001, A Paper Originally Prepared for the Center for Dewey Studies

Although I never had direct, personal contact with Makiguchi, he was the teacher of my own teacher, Josei Toda, and as such his philosophy and commitments have been a consistent presence in my life for more than half a century. During his long career as a primary school principal, he developed a unique theory of education that drew on his own teaching experience, his reading of contemporary educational theorists, including Dewey, and the Buddhism he embraced late in life.

During the final years of World War II, the Soka Kyoiku Gakkai (value-creating education society), the movement for educational, social and religious reform founded by Makiguchi and Toda, was violently suppressed by Japan's militarist authorities.

Makiguchi and Toda were jailed and Makiguchi died in prison at age seventy-three. Toda, surviving the ordeal, rebuilt the organization as a populist movement, the Soka Gakkai, based on the ideals of Buddhist humanism expounded by Makiguchi. My mentor's profound outrage against what he termed the "demonic nature of authority" — which had deprived Makiguchi of first his freedom, then his life — has been impressed indelibly on my being. It has driven my own determination to work for peace, for intercultural exchange and understanding, and for education.

Early Years in Meiji-era (1868–1912) Japan

Most of the extant photographs of Makiguchi show an expression that can best be characterized as stern. Those who interacted with him, however, have described him as warm and compassionate. Makiguchi's empathy and support, particularly for the downtrodden, can probably be traced to the sufferings of his youth. The process by which Japan transformed itself, in the last decades of the nineteenth century, from a feudal, largely agrarian society into a modern industrial power was accompanied by large-scale dislocation and disruption. Niigata Prefecture, where Makiguchi was born in 1871, felt these changes deeply. The supplanting of traditional Japan Sea trading routes sent once prospering communities into decline. Amidst extreme poverty, Makiguchi's father abandoned him at age three. His mother felt unable to care for him, and he was entrusted to relatives.

His efforts to continue his education were hampered by his adoptive family's poverty and the need to work to help support them. In 1885, at fourteen, he left home and moved to Japan's northernmost island of Hokkaido, where he found work as an errand boy in a police station. Recognizing his intellectual gifts, however, his supervisor supported Makiguchi's effort to attend a teachers' college, from which he graduated in 1893 at twenty-two. The fact that he had not graduated from a prestigious national university was one impediment to the acceptance of his ideas within the Japanese educational establishment, which then — as now — placed foremost emphasis on formal pedigree.

It was during Makiguchi's days as a young teacher that Japan began pursuing in earnest a policy of national wealth and military strength — the path of imperial expansion. In the field of education, highest priority was likewise accorded to national aims, and all efforts were made to instill a blind, unquestioning patriotism.

For example, in October 1890, the Japanese government had issued the Imperial Rescript on Education in the name of Emperor Meiji. This document served as a powerful instrument of political indoctrination and remained in effect until the end of World War II. Certified copies of the rescript were distributed to every school throughout the nation, and it was ceremoniously read at all important school events.

Students were required to study and memorize the text for their moral education classes. This 315-character text defined Japan's unique national polity based on the historical bonds uniting its benevolent rulers and their loyal subjects. It also stated as an imperative that all Japanese subjects should cultivate virtues, central among them being loyalty and filial piety for the greater glory of the imperial household. Makiguchi's assertion that the Emperor should not demand this loyalty was one of the charges listed in the indictment against him at the time of his arrest in 1943.

The Geography of Human Life

In 1903, at thirty-two, Makiguchi published his thousand-page work, *Jinsei Chirigaku* (The Geography of Human Life). Makiguchi's interest in geography, in particular, the interaction between and impact of geographical features and human activities, finds a parallel in Dewey's own thought. As Dewey wrote in *The School and Society*:

> The unity of all the sciences is found in geography. The significance of geography is that it presents the earth as the enduring home of the occupations of man. The world without its relationship to human activity is less than a world.[1]

Makiguchi's *Geography* was published on the eve of the Russo–Japanese War, as a result of which Japan emerged on the world stage as a major power. The tenor of the times is symbolized by the fact that seven of Japan's most famous scholars from Tokyo Imperial University petitioned the government to take a hard-line stance against Russia, heightening public enthusiasm for war. In contrast, Makiguchi sought to promote the ideal of global citizens who, while rooted in the local community, would avoid the pitfalls of "narrow-minded nationalism." He also compared imperialism to thievery on a grand scale,[2] the outcome of national egotism.[3]

Makiguchi, in the same work, declared that "the freedom and rights of the individual are sacred and inviolable."[4] It is important to note that the Japanese emperor had been granted supreme sovereignty and power by the 1889 Meiji Constitution, in which he was described using these same words, "sacred and inviolable." To appropriate this language, intimately linked to the emperor, for this distinctly democratic usage, was, in the context of his time, nothing less than audacious.

While Makiguchi was critical of what he termed "narrow-minded nationalism," he was also skeptical of "vacuous, utopian globalism" devoid of actual content. He posited a three-layered scheme of identity or citizenship; education should instill a sense of belonging and commitment to the community, to the nation, and to the world.[5] Ultimately, he saw the welfare of the world as intimately linked with and necessary to individual well-being. Years later, in 1941, when Japanese society was fully under the sway of virulent ultranationalism, Makiguchi would return again to the theme of the interdependent connections between the individual and the life of the world:

> Unless the ultimate aim is established, intermediate aims cannot be fixed. Without perceiving the world, one cannot understand the nation. Unless the life of the nation is realized, individual livelihood cannot be secured. Therefore, if we are to achieve stability of

individual livelihood in every household, that of the nation must first be established. Without the well-being of the world, that of a nation cannot be assured.[6]

Humanitarian Competition

Also in *The Geography of Human Life,* Makiguchi set forth his ideas about the path that human civilization had followed and the direction in which it should move. Influenced, like Dewey, by the Darwinian image of evolution, Makiguchi saw competition in its various forms as a driving force in history. Also like Dewey, Makiguchi never unquestioningly embraced the cult of progress but interrogated it from a variety of perspectives. He described the shifts over time in modes of national competition: from the military, to the political, to the economic — which he saw becoming, at the turn of the twentieth century, the predominant mode of competition.

Finally, moving from the descriptive to the predictive, he set out a vision of what he termed "humanitarian competition" — where he saw the future of his country and of humankind to lie. What Makiguchi described as humanitarian competition is not merely a locational or methodological shift in the competitive arena and modes. It represents a profound qualitative transformation in the very nature of competition, toward one that is based on a recognition of the interrelatedness and interdependence of human communities and that emphasizes the cooperative aspects of living.

He foresaw an age in which the power of character and the humane qualities of individuals and whole societies

— manifested in the creative forces of their cultural achievements — would be a greater force than military prowess, political or economic domination. He envisaged a time when people and countries would compete — in the original sense of "seeking together" — to make the greatest contribution to human happiness and well-being.

He also saw humanitarian competition influencing and transforming other modes of competition.

> The methods of humanitarian competition are not, of course, simple or unitary; all other forms of competition — military, political, economic — must be conducted within a humanitarian framework. In other words, the objective of states should not be merely the selfish pursuit of their own good, but should be to enhance the lives of other peoples as well. We must choose those methods that profit ourselves while profiting others. We must learn to engage consciously in collective life.[7]

This echoes Dewey's call for "drawing out and composing into a harmonious whole the best, the most characteristic which each contributing race and people has to offer."[8]

Toward the end of this work, and without much elaboration, Makiguchi wrote that he saw the first signs of humanitarian competition emerging in the United States. At the same time, he clearly hoped that Japan would choose the path of humanitarian competition.

Makiguchi saw a special role for island nations, which, being connected by oceans to the rest of the world, tend to act as points of contact, interaction and fusion among the world's cultures. He identified three island nations that he saw playing a pivotal role in the future of human civilization: Britain on the western edge of the Eurasian continent, Japan on the eastern flank, and the United States, which he considered an island nation writ large. Of these three, he saw the British Isles as already fulfilling the role of a cultural center; the United States was likewise destined, he felt, by location and by the multiple cultures it was embracing and absorbing, to become the future locus of human civilization. In Japan, he saw a similar potential and voiced his strong hope that this indeed would be the path Japan would choose to tread.

Geography closes with the hope that these three countries will make full use of their respective situations, propitious to the development of culture and the advancement of civilization, to engage in humanitarian competition for the benefit of the entire world.

Teaching Career and Educational Philosophy

In 1913, at age forty-two, Makiguchi was appointed principal of a primary school in Tokyo. For almost twenty years, he served in this capacity, assisting in the development of some of Tokyo's most outstanding public schools such as Shirogane and Taisho primary schools, at times even holding positions in two schools simultaneously.

As evidenced in his writing, Makiguchi was aware of Dewey's ideas and drew on them in his efforts to reform the Japanese educational system. In *The School and Society*, Dewey called for a Copernican revolution, by which the child becomes the center around which all educational endeavors must revolve.

Makiguchi likewise strove to make what we would now term "the best interests of the child" central to the theory and practice of education. He denounced the force-feeding of knowledge far removed from the realities of the child's everyday living. In its place, he called for education to have the happiness of children as its fundamental purpose. These sentiments can be sensed in the introduction to his 1930 work, *Soka kyoikugaku taikei* (The System of Value-Creating Pedagogy):

> I am driven by the intense desire to prevent the present deplorable situation — ten million of our children and students forced to endure the agonies of cutthroat competition, the difficulty of getting into good schools, the "examination hell" and the struggle for jobs after graduation — from afflicting the next generation. I therefore have no time to be concerned with the shift in vagaries of public opinion. . . .[9]

Indeed, Makiguchi was relentless in his critique of those social structures and authorities that accepted or actively promoted coercive and destructive modes of education. Makiguchi's views of education stood in sharp contrast to the prevailing nationalist agenda with its focus on raising "little national citizens." In *Pedagogy*, he asked: "What then is the purpose of national education? Rather than devise complex theoretical interpretations, it is better to start by looking to the lovely child who sits on your knee and ask yourself: What can I do to assure that this child will be able to lead the happiest life possible?"[10] Makiguchi's focus of interest was never the state but always people, individual human beings.

Pedagogy, incidentally, offers the one point of known, if indirect, contact between Makiguchi and Dewey in the form of a shared friend, Japanese diplomat and League of Nations Undersecretary-General Inazo Nitobe. Nitobe had encouraged Makiguchi's independent scholarship and wrote the foreword to *Pedagogy*, in which he described Makiguchi's views on education as representing a "major shift from the present idealistic approach to a genuine science of education." And it was Nitobe who played host to his longtime friend Dewey during his 1919 visit to Japan.

There was a strong preference in Japanese educational circles for high-minded conceptual theories and contempt for mere experience. In contrast, Makiguchi always stressed an experience-centered approach. He strongly asserted the importance of teachers assessing "cases of success and failure by analyzing their daily teaching experiences" as a basis for the discovery of principles.[11] In other words, he believed that principles should be extracted from experience and not imposed on reality "from above." Makiguchi's own ideas about education were derived directly from his experience as a teacher and school principal. The four volumes of *Pedagogy* (twelve were initially planned) were edited from the small mountain of notes he jotted on scraps of paper that he kept with him always for that purpose, sometimes even pausing in midconversation to set down a thought.

What he had observed and experienced as a teacher were widespread suffering and the tragic waste of human potential. His first posting as a teacher had been to a remote, rural region of Japan, where he taught in the Japanese equivalent of a one-room schoolhouse. The children were poor, and the manners they brought from their impoverished homes were rough.

Makiguchi, however, was insistent: "They are all equally students. From the viewpoint of education, what difference could there be between them and other students? Even though they may be covered with dust or dirt, the brilliant light of life shines from their soiled clothes. Why does no one try to see this? The teacher is all that stands between them and the cruel discrimination of society."[12]

In 1920, Makiguchi was assigned as the principal of a primary school in one of Tokyo's poorest neighborhoods. With the end of World War I, the demand for wartime production that had boosted the Japanese economy collapsed, and the unskilled laborers who were the parents of Makiguchi's pupils were forced to compete for meager employment opportunities. Moved by the spectacle of dire need, Makiguchi prepared box lunches — which he paid for out of his own pocket — for children whose families could not afford them, and in order not to hurt their feelings, he left them in the janitors' room for children to take them freely. This predated by many years the establishment of a formal school lunch program in Japan.

Confrontation with Educational Authorities

In Makiguchi's time, it was customary for principals to visit the wealthy and influential families in the school district, a practice he consistently refused to follow. Makiguchi also refused to accept the prevailing custom of granting special treatment to the children of influential families and encouraged teachers working under him to do likewise. When wealthy parents sought special treatment for their children, Makiguchi flatly refused.

In 1919, this stance came to the attention of a leading local politician, who lobbied for Makiguchi's removal. Students, teachers and parents all rallied to Makiguchi's defense and sought to have the transfer order stayed, even staging a three-day boycott of classes. Even after he had been transferred to another primary school, this same politician continued his campaign against Makiguchi. This time, Makiguchi made the educational authorities renovate a playground as a condition for accepting the transfer.

Because of these experiences, he insisted that it is crucial to create an inviolable realm for education, one protected from abuses of authority. To this end, he made a number of proposals in *The System of Value-Creating Pedagogy* and elsewhere. For example, he urged that an examination system be instituted for elementary school principals, to provide an objective, impartial basis for selection and to forestall selection of candidates with political or other connections. Also among Makiguchi's controversial proposals was a call to abolish the system of official inspection through which representatives of the central bureaucracy could directly interfere in the running of local schools.

Instead he advocated a democratic, participatory vision of education. He saw this as essential to assuring children's right to learn. He urged parents, and mothers especially, to become involved as active partners in their children's education. As mild as this may seem from the perspective of the present, it should be remembered that in Japan, until very recently, the standard expression for "parents" in relation to educational concerns has been *fukei* (lit. "fathers and elder brothers").

The Role of Teachers

What then is the concrete methodology of Makiguchi's value-creating education, and what roles does it suggest for teacher and learner? First, the emphasis shifts from education as the transmission of knowlege, a view that continues to predominate in Japan to this day, to education as the process of learning to learn. As Makiguchi put it:

> [Education] is not the piecemeal merchandising of information; it is the provision of keys that will allow people to unlock the vault of knowledge on their own. It does not consist in pilfering the intellectual property amassed by others through no additional effort of one's own; it would rather place people on their own path of discovery and invention.[13]

This quest for "discovery and invention" may be described as the learner's autonomous effort to discover and create value amidst the realities of life.

For teachers, this means several things. First, they must reassess their role as teachers.

> Teachers should come down from the throne where they are ensconced as the object of veneration to become public servants who offer guidance to those who seek to ascend the throne of learning. They should not be masters who offer themselves as paragons, but partners in the discovery of new models.[14]

The role suggested here bears resemblance to Socrates' metaphor of the educator as midwife or, as drawn by Friedrich Wilhelm August Fröbel, gardener. The emphasis in Makiguchi's pedagogy is not on teaching so much as the work of carefully guiding the students' own process of learning.

Thus teachers must be diligent in their efforts to deepen their understanding of how learning occurs. To this end, Makiguchi, like Dewey, urged a commitment to an empirical method.

> Positivism says that we are to take the daily realities before us in education as our working knowledge, then wield the scrupulous scalpel of the scientist to dissect out educational theory; that is, to yield the constant truths at the root of educational practice. Only then will education embrace an integrally systematized body of knowledge . . . .[15]

This also requires continuous learning and personal growth on the part of educators. Makiguchi himself was already past fifty when he took up the study of English with the help of a textbook designed for junior high school students.

Another anecdote comes to us from Masataka Kubota, a teacher at the Nishimachi Primary School in Tokyo where Makiguchi was principal in 1920:

> Having worked for a number of principals, there was nobody as devoted to learning as Mr. Makiguchi....
> The principal [Makiguchi] always had a newly published book in his hand, which he never monopolized, but always left for us to read, always inquiring after our impressions of the book.[16]

Philosophy of Value Creation

Central to Makiguchi's *Pedagogy* was his theory of value. In his schema, he modified the neo-Kantian value system of truth, goodness and beauty dominant in Japan at the time and reordered it as beauty, benefit (also translated as gain or utility) and goodness. He defined beauty as that which brings fulfillment to the aesthetic sensibility of the individual; benefit as that which advances the life of the individual in a holistic manner; goodness as that which contributes to the well-being of the larger human society.

While space does not permit a detailed analysis and comparison of Makiguchi's theory of value with Dewey's philosophy, a few points bear noting. Makiguchi removed "truth" from his list of values, seeing truth as essentially a matter of identification and correspondence; value, in contrast, is a measure of the subjective impact a thing or event has on our lives. While truth identifies an object's essential qualities or properties, value may be considered the measure of the relevance or impact an object or event bears on the individual. Makiguchi explains that:

> Value arises from the relationship between the evaluating subject and the object of evaluation. If either changes relative to the other, it is only obvious that the perceived value will change. The differences and shifts in ethical codes throughout history provide but one of the more outstanding proofs of the mutability of value.[17]

Dewey expresses a similar sense of historical and social contingency: "No longer will views generated in view of special situations be frozen into absolute standards and masquerade as eternal truths."[18] This aspect of Makiguchi's thought also parallels Dewey's critique of the centrality of epistemology in traditional philosophy and his focus on honing the tools of practical inquiry.

Following the suggestion of his young disciple, Josei Toda, Makiguchi coined the neologism *soka* for the creation (*sozo*) of value (*kachi*). The fundamental criterion for value, in Makiguchi's view, is whether something adds to or detracts from, advances or hinders, the human condition. This view resonates with what he found in Nichiren Buddhism, with its emphasis on manifesting one's innate human dignity amidst the challenges of everyday life. The humanistic philosophy of Buddhism provided a firm and animating foundation for his theory of value.

The theory of value and value-creation were central to the Soka Kyoiku Gakkai, which Makiguchi and Toda founded in 1930, with an initial membership of almost solely educators. At the time of its suppression by the authorities in 1943, the organization counted some three thousand members, from virtually all walks of life.

Through their various activities, members of the society sought to give form to Makiguchi's vision of education that would contribute to the lifelong happiness of learners. Firmly committed to the importance of "actual proof," these educators implemented the methods of value-creating education, recording and publicizing their results. As the organization's membership expanded and its activities shifted to a more purely religious focus, these same methods — of testing and proving — were applied to the realm of religious experience.

Experiential Learning for Global Citizenship

It was crucial, in both Dewey's and Makiguchi's view, to give children the opportunity to think and acquire experience in real-life settings.

This, of course, derived in Dewey's case from the philosophy of pragmatism, or as he preferred to term it, experimentalism. Contrary to the long-held view of experience as uncertain and anecdotal, Dewey reconceived experience as a fundamental, holistic function of life activity. Both Dewey and Makiguchi lamented the banishment of experience from the site of education. As Dewey describes it, the school was "so set apart, so isolated from the ordinary conditions and motives of life, ... [it] is the one place in the world where it is most difficult to get experience — the mother of all discipline...."[19] Makiguchi felt that the prevailing educational theories were "almost entirely unrelated to the realities of life."[20] He proposed a solution consonant in many ways with Dewey's own thinking.

> In-school education should be closely connected in practice with actual social life so that it can transform unconscious living into fully conscious participation in the life of society. Education integrated into the life of society will yield benefits of well-planned living, without the undesirable effect of mechanical uniformity, an inherent danger in standardized education.[21]

Dewey, linking school with everyday living, advocated the importance of guiding children to improve their social competence. In his words, a school should be a "genuine form of active community," "a miniature community, an embryonic society."[22] The essential aim of education implied here is the continuous, lifelong growth of an individual. This is brought about by acquiring experience, which evolves in depth and extensiveness from life in the home to that in school and finally to social life.

For his part, Makiguchi proposed a system in which students would attend class for a half day and spend the remaining half in "productive vocational activity," either assisting their parents' work, at a trade or further specialization of study. Makiguchi wanted this system to be implemented for all students from the primary to the university level. According to him, it would have the following merits: It would encourage greater efficiency in teaching (which Makiguchi was convinced from his own experiences was possible); make more effective use of limited educational facilities by effectively doubling the number of students who could receive education at a school; alleviate the "examination hell" by which students competed for access to those facilities; and, most critical in Depression-era Japan, produce graduates with experience and capabilities that would enhance their prospects of finding meaningful work.[23]

Both Makiguchi and Dewey were, in their respective social contexts, pointing to a prevailing weakness in education, the impact of which was visible in all aspects of society. As it was conceived, school could not prepare students to think critically about social conditions or contribute constructively to their improvement. Moreover, the traditional educational methods remained distant from the empirical, scientific approach that was proving so effective in other fields of human endeavor. Dewey's Laboratory School and Makiguchi's proposals, such as that for half-day schooling, can be thought of as attempts to close this gap, as well as the gap between living and learning, which was of deep concern to both. In Makiguchi's words, we should not view "learning as a preparation for living, but enable people to learn in the process of living."[24]

For a child operating under her own initiative, learning may be described as innovative, investigative as well as creative. To kindle in all children an ever-burning passion for discovery, one that will lead them unfailingly to think for themselves, make their own decisions and live out their lives accordingly — to do this is, in Makiguchi's view, to provide children the keys to the treasure house of knowledge.

Like Dewey, Makiguchi strove to realize a holistic approach to human development. For him, this meant enabling the student to engage in value creation, for which he set out six transformative indices. These are: from unconscious, emotional modes of living to a life of self-mastery, consciousness and rationality; from a life of less to one of greater value creation; from self-centered to a social and altruistic mode of living; from dependent to independent modes of living in which one is capable of making principle-based judgment; from a life dominated by external influences to a life of autonomy; from a life under the sway of desires to self-reflective modes of living in which one is capable of integrating one's actions into a larger sense of purpose.

Ultimately, he cherished a vision of fostering people who could be described as true global citizens — individuals fully able to transcend self-seeking egotism and elevate their way of life to one linked to all of humanity.

Drawing inspiration from Makiguchi's thinking and from the Buddhist understanding of interdependence, I offered the following goals for education for global citizenship at a talk I gave at Teachers College, Columbia University, in June 1996 (see pp. 112–13).

- The wisdom to perceive the interconnectedness of all life and living.

- The courage not to fear or deny difference but to respect and strive to understand people of different cultures and to grow from encounters with them.
- The compassion to maintain an imaginative empathy that reaches beyond one's immediate surroundings and extends to those suffering in distant places.

I am convinced that as we enter the twenty-first century, education that fosters these qualities is the most pressing imperative facing humankind.

In the Shadow of Totalitarianism

In 1939, the dark clouds of totalitarianism hung over the world. As Dewey warned in his *Freedom and Culture:*

> Democratic ends demand democratic methods for their realization. . . .
> [R]ecourse to monistic, wholesale, absolutist procedures is a betrayal of human freedom no matter in what guise it presents itself.[25]

Japan was by this time fully caught up in the vortex of totalitarianism. Needless to say, neither the means nor the objectives were democratic.

The Japanese people had been manipulated into supporting the goals of imperial aggression and expansion in Asia under the guise of creating a "Greater East Asia Co-Prosperity Sphere." This slogan, purporting pan-Asian coexistence and co-prosperity, was Japan's justification for replacing Western colonial imperatives and influence with its own.

In 1938, the National Mobilization Law stripped people of their civil rights and granted summary powers of government over national resources, both human and material. In the name of national defense, the entire nation was mobilized. In April 1939, the government enacted the Religious Organizations Law. This law empowered the government to disband any religious organization whose teachings or activities contradicted the "Imperial Way."

In 1941, the Peace Preservation Act of 1925 was revised, expanding its scope to prohibit — under penalty of life imprisonment or death — any acts that were seen as blasphemous of the emperor or of State Shinto, which asserted the emperor's divinity.

Makiguchi chose this time to launch a frontal critique of militarist fascism. At the time, most religions and religious organizations in Japan lent their support to State Shinto, which provided the philosophical and spiritual underpinnings for the prosecution of the war. Makiguchi, who had embraced Nichiren Buddhism in 1928, opposed this trampling underfoot of the freedoms of conscience and belief. Again and again, in writing and in speech, he criticized the government's stance. To the end, he refused to compromise his commitment to peace.

In 1941, the guiding principles of the Soka Kyoiku Gakkai were published in the first issue (July 21) of the organization's journal *Kachi Sozo* (Value Creation). Here, Makiguchi sought to express a balance between what he had long identified as the destructive aspects of unrestrained individualism and the totalitarian ethos that was sweeping Japan.

> The Soka Kyoiku Gakkai shall be a gathering devoted neither to the individualism dictated by a myopic worldview that ignores the welfare of others nor the fallacious dictates of totalitarianism that divests the individual of his identity. Instead, it shall take as its highest honor to be a living testimony to a truly holistic way of life that is based on a correct and undistorted worldview.[26]

In the spring of 1942, *Kachi Sozo* was forced to cease publication at the order of the domestic security authorities.

Japan's military authorities were constantly vigilant against any sign of independence of opinion. They systematically undermined freedom of thought, conscience and expression in their efforts to make the populace an obedient, sheeplike mass. Makiguchi expressed his firm conviction that "a single lion will triumph over a thousand sheep. A single person of courage can achieve greater things than a thousand cowards."[27]

In Makiguchi's theory of value, discussed earlier, good and evil are understood as relational. In many of his later writings, Makiguchi is harshly critical of what he termed "small good" — the passive avoidance of evil. He is insistent that "great good" could be realized only by confronting and challenging "great evil" — which he clearly identified as the actions and belief structures of militarist Japan.

As a result of these attitudes, Makiguchi was targeted as a "thought criminal," and his activities were subject to constant surveillance by the secret police.

Nevertheless, Makiguchi continued to organize small discussion meetings where he openly expressed his religious and moral convictions. According to his written indictment, he attended over the course of two wartime years more than 240 such meetings in different parts of Japan. In the presence of the police during these meetings, Makiguchi continued to criticize military fascism. Often his speech would be cut short by the police.

In November 1942, Makiguchi addressed the Fifth General Meeting of the Soka Kyoiku Gakkai. In that speech, he praised as "an incontrovertible truth" Dewey's assertion that our chosen way of living can only be proven within and through the act of actual living. The record of this meeting proved to be the last official publication of the Soka Kyoiku Gakkai.

In July 1943, Makiguchi and Toda were arrested by the dreaded Special Higher Police. *Tokko Geppo* (Monthly Report of the Special Higher Police) reports the arrest of Makiguchi: "The thoughts and beliefs of [Soka Kyoiku Gakkai]-related persons centering on President Makiguchi manifest a number of subversive and seditious elements. Following secret investigations by the Police Agency as well as the Fukuoka Prefecture Special Higher Police Department, the Agency on the seventh day of this month arrested and interrogated Tsunesaburo Makiguchi and five other persons for suspicion of blaspheming the dignity of the Imperial Grand Shrine and lèse majesté." Makiguchi was charged with expressing such opinions as: "The emperor is a common mortal"; "The emperor should not demand the people's loyalty"; and "There is no need to worship the Grand Shrine of Ise," a sacred site with close ties to the imperial household.[28]

Makiguchi was already seventy-two and spent the next year and four months, a total of 500 days, in solitary confinement. Throughout, he refused to recant. Rather, he engaged in courageous dialogue with his interrogators and fellow prisoners, sharing with them the convictions for which he had been arrested. His stance remained, to the very end, one of a humanistic educator, committed to his own beliefs and opposed to the direction in which Japan was headed.

For example, under questioning, Makiguchi describes the ongoing war as a "national disaster" — not a "holy war" as it was officially characterized — that had been brought about by adherence to erroneous ideologies. He also repeated his assertion that the Japanese emperor is neither divine nor infallible.[29]

On November 18, 1944, he succumbed to the ravages of privation and brutal treatment, a martyr to the cause of human freedom and dignity.

Views of Religion

As mentioned above, Makiguchi was already fifty-seven when he embraced Nichiren Buddhism, an advanced age for an enthusiastic religious conversion. Dewey, having let lapse his ties to any specific church, sought to pursue religion as an impulse and experience ("the religious") outside the framework of any particular tradition. Makiguchi, in apparent contrast, adopted a lineage of Buddhism traceable to a specific teacher — in this case the thirteenth-century monk Nichiren. Despite this difference, their approach to religion and the function of religious faith are in fact deeply cognate.

First, both were adamant that religion must serve humanity; humanity does not exist to serve religion. Emblematic of this, Makiguchi rejected the neo-Kantian Wilhelm Windelband's positing of the sacred as an independent category of value. Rather, he held that religion, to the degree it enhances the lives of individuals, generates the value of benefit or gain; and to the degree it contributes to the advancement of society, creates the value of good. Beyond this, in Makiguchi's view, religion had no purpose. This refusal to acknowledge "the sacred" as a self-sufficient value and his insistence that religion has value only to the degree that it concretely advances the human condition is deeply resonant with Dewey's rejection of the supernatural and his understanding of "the religious" as that which can "unify interests and energies now dispersed; it can direct action, generate the heat of emotion and the light of intelligence."[30]

Further, it should be noted that Makiguchi's embrace of Nichiren Buddhism was the outcome of a highly conscious process. His commitment to an empirical method of evaluation and choice-making was so deep as to preclude anything resembling blind faith or dogmatism.

This is illustrated by Makiguchi's own journey of faith. Born to a Zen Buddhist family and having close Christian friends, Makiguchi had gained exposure to a number of religious traditions. Although he felt that none of these faiths withstood the test of scientific and philosophical inquiry, he refused to dismiss religion *per se* as meaningless.

In 1928, as he was preparing the first volume of *Pedagogy*, Makiguchi began to study the key Mahayana Buddhist text, the Lotus Sutra. Here he was struck by a sense that the Sutra, and its interpretation by Nichiren, accorded fully with his own rational principles.

This was not his first exposure to Nichiren. His foster family had practiced a form of Nichiren Buddhism, and he had attended the lectures of Chigaku Tanaka whose interpretation of Nichiren's teachings was highly nationalistic and emperor-centered. Makiguchi appears to have been unimpressed by Tanaka's ideas, and they played no role in shaping his own later reception of Nichiren's teachings. When Makiguchi re-encountered Nichiren Buddhism, this time in the form of the more humanist/pacifist reading of fellow educator Sokei Mitani, he found a system of religious thought that "revitalized" his theory of value.[31]

As a philosophy, Buddhism accords central importance to life. As Nichiren stated: "Life is the foremost of all treasures. It is expounded that even the treasures of the entire major world system cannot equal the value of one's body and life."[32] This clearly resonated with Makiguchi's own views: "The only value in the true sense is that of life itself. All other values arise solely within the context of interaction with life."[33] Both Buddhism and Makiguchi's philosophy contain a powerful critique of the prevailing militarist ideology that saw the lives of individual citizens and soldiers as subservient to — and expendable in — the overriding interests of the state.

From his writings, it is clear that Makiguchi saw the Soka Kyoiku Gakkai as a lay movement dedicated to realizing a "life of great good" through the practice of Nichiren Buddhism. As he is recorded saying during his police interrogation, his decision not to become a priest but to remain a lay practitioner stemmed from his desire not to be confined within a narrow sectarian interpretation of Buddhism.[34] Makiguchi clearly saw himself as returning to the core values of Buddhism, most notably a prioritization of human life and happiness, while at the same time developing ideational and organizational structures that could put these into practice in the twentieth century.

Specifically, the aspects of Nichiren Buddhism he found attractive were: 1) an emphasis on empirical experience and congruence with the scientific method; 2) the centrality of a universal law or principle (dharma) as the focus of faith rather than an anthropomorphic being or deity; and 3) an emphasis on social engagement and a stance of using religion's contribution to society as the measure of its validity.

Regarding the second aspect, the emphasis on the law over the person, Makiguchi felt that this was a mode of faith consonant with the historical trend toward constitutional democracy under an impartial rule of law, as opposed to rule by the despotic will of a single individual. "Rely on the law, not the person" is one of the famous injunctions of Buddhism, which Makiguchi repeated consistently. The law, in Buddhism, is the law of causality, of cause and effect.

This law, according to Makiguchi:

is not confined to the physical present nor to the linear span of a single lifetime. It presides over humanity for time without end, in the boundless expanse of space and time, in the spiritual and the material realms. We live in its midst; we are inevitably subject to this law of causality.[35]

A Universal Law of Causality

Needless to say, the gulf between Makiguchi's principle-based view of religion and the dominant ideology in militarist Japan was vast. Starting in the 1920s, the government took an increasingly active interest in the religious beliefs and practices of its citizens. A series of ever-more stringent laws were passed restricting heterodox views and seeking to unify the spiritual resources of the nation under State Shinto. During the 1930s, several large sects were violently suppressed and their membership dispersed.

The structures of the militarist state were intimately intertwined with State Shinto, which forged from the indigenous animism of Japan an ideology of nationalism centered on the purity and "selection" of the Japanese race and the divinity of the emperor. Imperialist Japan not only enforced this belief system domestically but sought to forcibly export it. This disgusted Makiguchi who declared: "The arrogance of the Japanese people knows no bounds."[36]

To question any aspect of this ideology was to challenge the legitimacy of Japanese militarism, its policies and their impact. The state became increasingly intolerant of dissent as the military position of Japan in the war became increasingly desperate. As stated, the Peace Preservation Act strictly outlawed any act or statement that could be construed as criticizing Japanese "unique national polity" (*rokutai*). It thus required enormous courage on Makiguchi's part to write, in the December 1941 Soka Kyoiku Gakkai periodical *Kachi Sozo* (Value Creation):

> We must strictly avoid following ideologies of uncertain origin that cannot be substantiated by actual proof — even if they may be the most time-honored tradition — and thereby sacrificing the precious lives of ourselves and others. In this sense, the question of [compulsory worship at] Shinto shrines must be rethought as a matter of great urgency.[37]

Again, Makiguchi returned to his belief in the all-pervasive Buddhist law of causality, rather than the caprices of individuals. He extended this outlook even to his understanding of Shakyamuni, the Buddha. Makiguchi is recorded as responding to his police interrogators as follows:

> Buddhism is not something invented or created by Shakyamuni. Without beginning or end, it is a law governing and giving vitality to the constant flow of all phenomena since time without beginning. What is called Buddhism are simply acts and practices that accord with this already existing law or principle.[38]

To understand the nature of this law is to understand Buddhism and at the same time Makiguchi's philosophy, a philosophy of value creation that continues to inspire millions of people worldwide. In Makiguchi's view — and that of Buddhism — the ultimate "law" is neither transcendent nor anthropomorphic. It does not exist behind or above reality but within it. As Nichiren explained in an exegesis on a sutra passage: "'no worldly affairs of life or work are ever contrary to the true reality.' A person of wisdom is not one who practices Buddhism apart from worldly affairs...."[39]

It was this commitment to reality, to experience, to people and to the work of finding real-life solutions to the problems of living that sustained Makiguchi in his final confrontation with the Japanese militarist state. These same elements have been inherited and given concrete form in the global activities of the membership of the Soka Gakkai International.

In Conclusion

Although denied recognition during his lifetime, Makiguchi's intellectual and spiritual legacy has had an important impact in Japan and beyond. In the postwar years, the organization Makiguchi founded was reconstituted as the Soka Gakkai by his disciple, Josei Toda, growing into a Buddhist-based grassroots movement with membership in the millions. Today the Soka Gakkai International has active members in some 163 [editor's note: as of 2010, the number is 192] countries worldwide and is involved in peace education, environmental protection and the promotion of international understanding through cultural exchange. Makiguchi's theories have begun to attract the serious interest of educators throughout the world.

It is also these same values — reality, experience, people — that form the most solid link between Makiguchi and the pragmatic philosophy of John Dewey. Inevitably, the course of their lives and careers, as well as the impact they exerted on their respective societies, diverge widely. But for just this reason, it is inspiring to learn from the lives of two men whose ideas and commitments developed along parallel paths united by a profound desire to contribute to human happiness, in particular the happiness of children.

Today, what our world requires most is a vast, collaborative effort by all those who share a commitment to empowering children and young people with the inner means for a lifetime of growth, happiness and the creation of value. Toward this end, and inspired by the examples of these great men and others like them, I believe we must continue our efforts without cease.

PART ONE

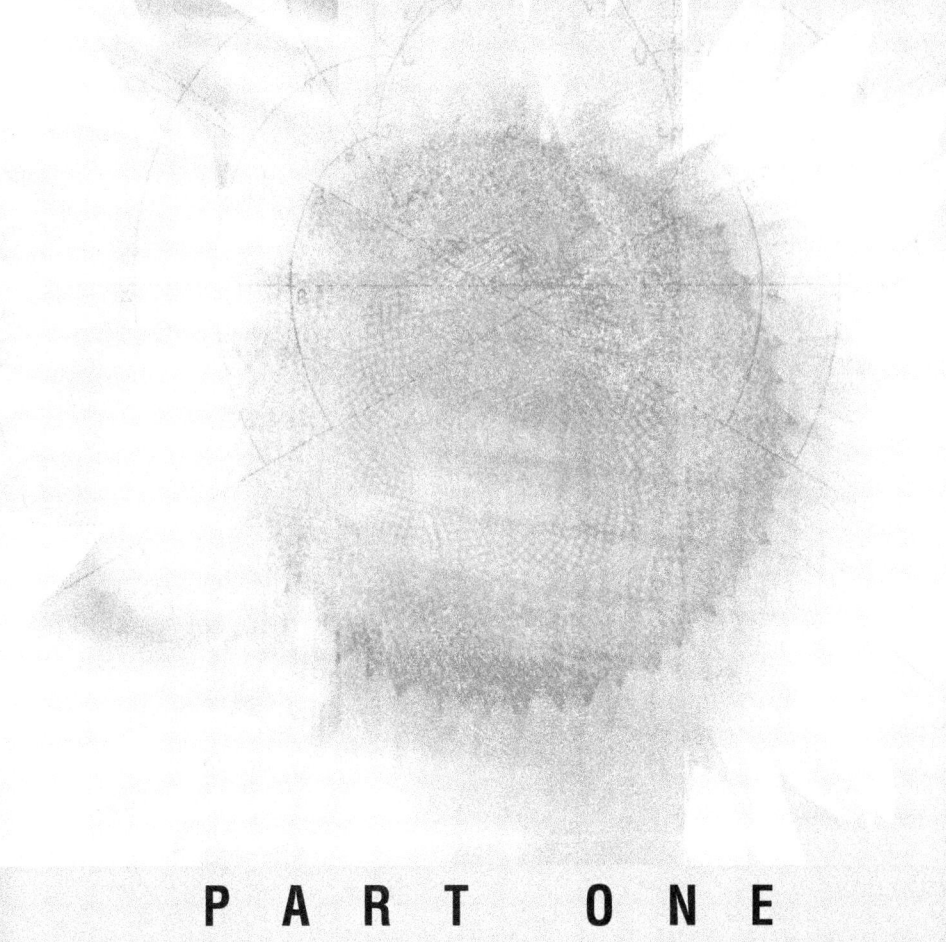

Addresses and Proposals

1

The Challenge of Global Empowerment: Education for a Sustainable Future

On the occasion of the 2002 World Summit on Sustainable Development, August 26–September 4, 2002

The Need for Change

More than ten years have passed since the holding of the Earth Summit[1] in Brazil, an event that sparked sharply increased awareness of the need to protect the global environment. Since then, the term *sustainable development* has become an integral part of our vocabulary, and on certain fronts progress has been made. Overall, however, the agreements reached in Rio have not been kept and the progress that has been made is not keeping pace with the degradation of Earth's life systems. It is clear that we cannot permit this situation to continue further into the twenty-first century.

Resolving this crisis will require the commitment of more knowledge, technology and funds. But what is even more fundamentally lacking in my view are such intangible elements as a sense of solidarity and common purpose with our fellow inhabitants of Earth and a real sense of responsibility toward future generations.

In June of 2002, I had the opportunity to meet with Mr. Tommy E. Remengesau Jr., president of the Republic of Palau, an island nation often described as a jewel set in the Pacific Ocean. At that time, we discussed the environmental crisis, and President Remengesau shared his deep concerns.

"Global warming," he said, "is an extremely serious issue for the people of Palau. Ocean levels have risen and salt water is invading the aquifers. The natural beauty of our islands is threatened. El Niño has caused the rains to fail, and the destruction of our coral reefs is progressing. Greatly increased water temperature has caused the coral to turn white and die...." The president also mentioned that Palau is actively engaged in researching and introducing alternative energy sources that reduce greenhouse gases.

The times demand this kind of active response—this refusal to be a passive observer or victim of circumstances—not only at the governmental level but also at the grassroots level of civil society.

In the film *A Quiet Revolution,* which was produced by the Earth Council specifically for the 2002 World Summit on Sustainable Development, inspiring examples of such action are presented. These include people's responses to the problem of water resources in Nimi Village in India and to the threat of persistent organic pollutants in Zemplinska Sirava lake in Slovakia, as well as the example of women who have stood up to protect the forests of Kenya.

Our organization, the Soka Gakkai International, supporting the objectives of this film, cooperated in its production. This is because we believe that the theme running through the film—that a single person can change the world—is the message of courage and hope most needed in these difficult times.

One of the goals of the WSSD was to adopt a plan of implementation that will serve as the basis for making the twenty-first century an era of creative coexistence between humans and nature. UN Secretary-General Kofi Annan had emphasized that the summit would serve as a litmus test for countries' resolve to act.

As part of our efforts to support the WSSD, I offered, in a proposal written earlier in 2002, three suggestions for possible reform of the international system relating to protection of the environment. The first was the appointment of a UN high commissioner for the environment to exercise clear leadership and initiative on global environmental problems. The second was the phased consolidation of the secretariats overseeing the implementation of various environmental treaties, linked to the establishment of a global green fund. The third was the adoption of a convention for the promotion of renewable energy resources.

At the same time, I stressed the need to raise consciousness and change our basic ways of thinking about the environment. In addition to "top-down" reforms, such as the legal and institutional measures outlined above, any lasting solution will require commensurate "bottom-up" reforms that build and strengthen solidarity at the people's level. These are the two interlinked prerequisites of change on a global scale. In this proposal, I would like to focus on the question of how to forge global popular solidarity toward resolution of the global environmental crisis.

International Decade of Education for Sustainable Development

If people are to take environmental issues as their personal concern and harmonize their efforts for our common future, education is vital. Only education can provide the driving force for such a renewal of awareness. For this reason, the SGI put forward the idea of an international decade of education for sustainable development to follow the UN Decade for Human Rights Education from the year 2005. This proposal was included in the plan of implementation adopted in Johannesburg and, in December 2002, it was approved by the UN General Assembly with UNESCO named as the coordinating agency. The objectives of the decade would be to promote education as the basis for a sustainable human society and to strengthen international cooperation toward the dissemination of environmental information.

The importance of education for sustainable development was clearly stated in the Agenda 21 plan of action adopted at the 1992 Earth Summit in Rio de Janeiro. At the heart of this concept—as stressed in the 1997 Thessaloniki Declaration of the International Conference on Environment and Society—is sustainability.

In the words of the declaration: "The concept of sustainability encompasses not only environment but also poverty, population, health, food security, democracy, human rights and peace." Because environmental issues are so deeply interlinked with these other global issues, their resolution requires a fundamental rethinking of our way of life—as individuals, as societies and in terms of human civilization itself.

In this sense, I believe the decade of education for sustainable development should be promoted with the following three goals in mind:

- To learn and deepen awareness of environmental issues and realities.
- To reflect on our modes of living, renewing these toward sustainability.
- To empower people to take concrete action to resolve the challenges we face.

To Learn

It is essential to deepen understanding and awareness. Everything starts from grasping basic facts: for example, the amount of the world's forests that have been lost; the degree of pollution of the air, water and soil; and the overall impact on the global ecosystem.

We also need to understand the causes and social structures driving environmental destruction. And beyond that, we need to learn to empathetically understand the realities of those who suffer, embracing their pain as our own and conscious of our interconnectedness. Such an effort will give birth to renewed awareness and determination to act.

It is vital to incorporate such efforts particularly into the early years of the school curriculum, the stage of growth when children are most rich in their sensitivity, imagination and creativity, when their desire to learn and absorb is at its height. A number of countries already promote environmental education as an integral part of their school curriculum. To cultivate in children's hearts the desire to treasure nature and protect the Earth is a vital step toward protecting their future.

At Kansai Soka Junior High School in Japan, students have been participating in experiential learning, filming the Earth from the space shuttle and international space station as part of NASA's EarthKAM[2] program. As founder of the school, I have been moved and impressed by the educational impact of the children visually confirming evidence of the global environmental crisis through this process.

For some years, I have called for a World Summit of Educators that would bring together not only those responsible for educational policy in each country but also those engaged on the front lines of education. The start of the decade of education for sustainable development (2005) would, I feel, be an appropriate time to hold an international conference where educators from throughout the world can exchange ideas, experiences and best practices in this area.

At the same time, it is also important that grassroots movements develop opportunities that encourage a deeper understanding of the global environmental crisis. It was to this end that the SGI organized the exhibition "Toward a Century of Hope: Environment and Development" as an official event of the Earth Summit in Rio. In the United States, the SGI-USA has created a traveling exhibition titled "Ecology and Human Life" and the Soka Gakkai in Japan has developed the "EcoAid" exhibition. These efforts, held in cooperation with other NGOs, seek to contribute to public education and enhance awareness at the grassroots.

To Reflect

Together with the provision of accurate information, it is crucial that the ethical values we share are clarified. This is particularly important in the case of environmental issues, which can be so vast and complex that information and knowledge alone can leave people without a clear sense of what concrete steps they can take, wondering what this all means to them. To counter such feelings of powerlessness and disconnection, education should encourage understanding of the ways that environmental problems intimately connect to our daily lives. Education must also inspire the faith that each of us has both the power and the responsibility to effect positive change on a global scale.

The Thessaloniki Declaration states: "Sustainability is, in the final analysis, a moral and ethical imperative in which cultural diversity and traditional knowledge need to be respected." We can learn from the rich spiritual heritage and diverse cultural traditions humanity has fostered over history. From these we can gain precious lessons and philosophical insights into how best to live as human beings.

The Earth Charter—whose drafting was initiated by the secretary-general of the Earth Summit in Rio, Maurice Strong, and Green Cross International President Mikhail Gorbachev—compiles and melds together these many different sources of wisdom. Its four pillars are: 1) respect for all life, 2) ecological integrity, 3) social and economic justice and 4) democracy, non-violence and peace. The Earth Charter offers a comprehensive overview of the values and principles needed for a sustainable future and as such it is an invaluable educational resource.

In addition to its content, the manner in which this "people's charter" was drafted is significant. In the drafting process, efforts were made to incorporate the essential wisdom of cultures and traditions from all regions of Earth. The language of the drafts was patiently deliberated by experts as well as by many people at the grassroots. To date, the SGI has held workshops and symposiums around the world in an effort to promote and introduce the Earth Charter principles at the grassroots level. I hope that many efforts would be made to learn from the Earth Charter, in programs that link its principles to the specific issues of different communities and their schools.

One of the themes of the Kenyan Green Belt Movement[3] is that the desert does not come from the Sahara—it begins in our backyards. Based on a sense of responsibility toward the future, mothers and children involved in the movement have planted and cared for some 20 million trees (between 1977 and 2002). I understand that children who have planted trees often enjoy friendly competition, pouring their love and concern onto the saplings, vying to see whose will grow fastest. Efforts such as this are very significant because it is through such experiences that people—young people in particular—come to grasp the concrete realities of their community and sharpen their awareness of the global environment.

The founder of the Soka Gakkai, the Japanese educator Tsunesaburo Makiguchi, described the local community as the world in miniature. He stressed the importance of opening children's eyes to the world through learning rooted in the local community—the place where history, nature and society intersect.

I believe that this kind of cyclical movement—viewing the world from the perspective of the local community, looking at the community through the lens of the world—is vital if we are to develop an ethical understanding and appreciation of nature that is truly rooted in the felt realities of daily life.

To Empower

Third, people must be empowered with courage and hope if they are to take those first concrete steps. Even if we establish agreed-upon ethics and paradigms of behavior, unless an increasing number of people embody and practice these in their lives, the severe realities we face will not change. In other words, if ethics bear little connection to our individual lives or will, but are seen as merely a set of guidelines to be passively followed, an obligation imposed from without, they will not enable us to respond robustly to changing circumstances. They will be abandoned in the first crisis.

It is for this reason that environmental ethics must be felt as a deeply personal vow and pledge, the fulfillment of which provides us with an inexhaustible sense of purpose and joy.

I recently engaged in a dialogue, through meetings and correspondence, with the environmental economist and futurist Dr. Hazel Henderson. She has spoken of her own inspiration to act, drawn from her efforts to protect her daughter from the hazards of air pollution.

"Most of us who started to work on the 'Citizens for Clean Air' campaign were mothers," she said. "Since we knew what a big task bringing children up is, we were anxious for our children to have the best futures possible. Thinking back, I realize that's what gave us the strength to endure all kinds of persecution and see the fight through to the end."

To be effective, ethics must be charged with this kind of natural and spontaneous sentiment—the irresistible impulse to act that moves us when we see the people and the world we love exposed to danger. Living ethics such as these are truly integrated into the very fiber of our humanity.

What, then, are the values that can serve to truly unite humanity, to link ordinary citizens in genuine solidarity? At the very heart of the values we seek must be a profound reverence for life itself. Such a sense of respect and reverence can awaken people to a sense of connection with all the forms of life with which we currently share this Earth, as well as a sense of oneness with future generations.

This appreciation of the unity and connectedness of life has been a part of many cultural traditions since ancient times; it has been passed on and continues today in many indigenous cultures. It is vital that humanity as a whole humbly attend to this living wisdom. For example, the Desana of the Amazon say that human beings cannot live in isolation and only thrive when they are in harmonious coexistence with their environment. The Iroquois of North America exhort us to make all decisions keeping in view "not only the present but also the coming generations, even those whose faces are yet beneath the surface of the ground—the unborn of the future." In this worldview, all animals and plants are seen as siblings.

A Contributive Way of Life

This reverence for life is also stressed in many religious traditions. In the Buddhist tradition that inspires the activities of the SGI, we find these words: "May all beings, those who can be seen and those who cannot be seen, those who live far away and those who live nearby, those who have been born and those still desiring to be born, may all living beings enjoy happiness!"

These words are rooted in the view that all life is interconnected and mutually supporting—a relationship described as "dependent origination" in Buddhism. What is key here is the understanding that the desire for happiness lies at the very heart of our interconnection. It is for this reason the teachings of Buddhism stress our role as the protagonists of positive change. While recognizing the influence that our surroundings have on us, the focus is more on our active and conscious engagement with our environment and with other forms of life. The powerful will that drives this dynamic process of change is the concern and compassion we muster for others.

Through dialogue and engagement, we draw forth and inspire in ourselves and in the lives of others a profound sense of purpose and joy. We begin a process of fundamental change that awakens a vastly expanded sense of identity—our "greater self." The ultimate objective of the SGI's activities—starting with a reformation, or *human revolution*, in our individual lives—is to bring about a universal flowering of the philosophy of reverence for life.

In his 1930 book, *The Pedagogy of Value-Creating Education*, Tsunesaburo Makiguchi called for a fundamental transformation in the way people live their lives. He decried a passive, dependent way of life and declared that even an active, independent way of life is insufficient. Instead he called for a consciously interactive, interdependent mode of existence, a life of committed contribution.

A passive and dependent way of life lacks a clearly defined sense of self; we live at the mercy of changing circumstances. An independent mode of living may manifest a clear sense of individual self but lack awareness of the realities and needs of others. In contrast, a contributive way of life is based on an awareness of the interdependent nature of our lives—of the relationships that link us to others and our environment. It is a way of life in which we actively strive to realize happiness both for ourselves and for others.

Such a way of life is centered on what we now call *empowerment*, in particular through the kind of dialogue that unleashes our vast inner potential, inspiring people to work together for the peace and happiness of the entire global community.

Here I am reminded of the words of Aurelio Peccei, cofounder of the Club of Rome, whose report *The Limits to*

Growth awakened the world to the environmental crisis. In a dialogue we shared, Dr. Peccei stated: "The gamut of still dormant capacities available in each individual is so great that we can make of them the greatest human resource. It is by grooming and developing these capacities in a way consistent with our new condition in this changed world—and only in this way—that we can again put a modicum of order and harmony in our affairs, including our relations with Nature, and thus move safely ahead."

Nothing is more crucially important today than the kind of humanistic education that enables people to sense the reality of interconnectedness, to appreciate the infinite potential in each person's life, and to cultivate that dormant human potential to the fullest.

No matter how complex global challenges may seem, we must remember that it is we ourselves who have given rise to them. It is therefore impossible that they are beyond our power as human beings to resolve. Refocusing on humanity, reforming and opening up the inner capacities of our lives — this kind of individual human revolution can enable effective reform and empowerment on a global scale.

To express my heartfelt wishes for the successful implementation of all the plans agreed upon at the WSSD (2002), I would like to share these words of my dear late friend the poet laureate of Denmark Dame Esther Gress.

>*If you want to change the world*
>*you must change man.*

*If you want to change man
you must make him want to change.*
—Esther Gress

And I would like to offer these words of the renowned Nigerian writer Ben Okri from his poem dedicated to the new century.

*You can't remake the world
Without remaking yourself.
Each new era begins within.
It is an inward event,
With unsuspected possibilities
For inner liberation.*
—Ben Okri

2

Reviving Education

January 9, 2001

The twenty-first century is upon us at last. Out of a desire to see this new century become one of education, I presented a paper on education in the autumn of 2000. My aim was twofold: to sound the alarm in Japan over the continuing treatment of education as simply a means to an end, and to call for a shift from viewing education as serving the narrowly defined needs of society to a new paradigm that sees society serving the lifelong process of education.

I believe it is vital that education be reoriented to its prime objective, namely, the lifelong happiness of learners. In this paper, I wish to delve further into the problems of education against which schools and society must be vigilant if we are to find a solution to the bullying and other acts of violence that most immediately and directly affect children.

Incidents of bullying and other forms of physical and psychological violence have been on the rise for some time in Japan, despite the ideal of schools being havens of the joys of learning and living. The Ministry of Education's 1999 survey of public schools from elementary through high-school levels reported a record 36,000 incidents of violent behavior, the highest to date. And although the numbers appear to be on a slightly downward trend, there were well over 30,000 cases of physical and psychological bullying reported.

This suggests a deplorable situation. Since the numbers do not hint at how many incidents go unreported, let alone how many occur in private schools, some observers claim reported incidents represent merely the tip of the iceberg.

Scrutiny of the numbers aside, the point here is that aberrant conditions have become the norm. Children are the microcosm of the times, and, as such, they mirror the future of society. As long as these mirrors remain dark and clouded, we will not see in them a hope-filled future.

While some remedial measures have been instituted by the Ministry of Education and independent commissions, I feel that along with structural deterrents to bullying there is an urgent need to establish not only in schools but throughout society an ethos of zero tolerance toward violence.

An Earnest Wish to End Violence

Tsunesaburo Makiguchi, the Japanese educator and first president of the Soka Gakkai, lamented the plight of the children of his day whose education and very lives bore the imprint of the march toward imperial expansion. This was a man who cherished a deep desire to resolve the underlying problems causing intense suffering to an entire generation of ten million children and students exposed to the pressures of a society in turmoil. He was determined that the burden of these problems not be passed on to the next generation.[1] From this vow was born his key work on education, *Soka kyoikugaku taikei* (The System of Value-Creating Pedagogy), published more than seventy years ago in 1930. Central to his formulation of Soka, or value-creating, education is the tenet that all children should be afforded the opportunity to develop their potential limitlessly and to lead fulfilling lives undeterred by the destructive influences in society. This tenet continues to be the driving force of the Soka schools today.

We must end the tragedy of school violence whereby the rich seeds of future promise and potential are destroyed by the children themselves. Every time I visit the Soka schools in Tokyo and Kansai, I speak frankly with the students, stating that bullying and violence are in all cases wrong, and encouraging the students that we should all work together to eliminate these evils from society.

Of course, my appeal to the students is not particularly novel. For the vast majority of the adult population, there is a common-sense assumption that the rejection of violence is a cornerstone of civilized society. Unfortunately, of late it seems we can no longer assume this to be the norm of social behavior. While documented incidents of school violence and other acts of juvenile crime and misconduct may not have dramatically increased in recent years, the problem is not defined simply by the frequency of its occurrence. Rather, we must examine closely the specific nature of the problem. Unless we squarely face this reality, any appeal to end bullying will fall short of reaching children's hearts and, instead, have the hollow ring of a superficial slogan.

Above all, we need courage if we are to end violence in schools — the kind of courage that will allow us neither to yield when confronted by evil nor to remain idle witnesses in the face of evil. When we muster up this kind of courage, bullying as well as all other forms of violence will inevitably be rejected. The question is whether we can indeed summon this courage. On the subject of bullying, last year the *Seikyo Shimbun* (the Soka Gakkai's daily newspaper) published a series of discussions between myself and several young people regularly in contact with junior high school students. From these talks I became acutely aware of how difficult it is — for parents and teachers as well as for students — to be truly courageous individuals.

Aversion to Good, Aversion to Evil

The philosopher and religious writer Simone Weil astutely observed that for writers of her day "words which contain a reference to good and evil" had become "degraded, especially those which refer to the good."[2] We see this increasingly in our own time, when words related to *good* — not only *courage* but also *effort, patience, love* and *hope* — are met with cynicism and indifference. Ours is a social climate in which people are perhaps fearful of being judged by others and hesitate even to utter such words. Unless we boldly confront cynicism and indifference, we cannot make fundamental and effective responses.

This undercurrent of social and spiritual malaise has spread rapidly in recent years. The question, "Why is it wrong to kill people?" was asked recently on a popular Japanese television program. It then became the title of a feature series in a magazine and was later published as a book.³ These phenomena give us an indication of where the problem lies: When even the time-honored tenets and virtues articulated in all the major world religions, such as prohibitions against the taking of human life, are called into question, one can easily imagine the prevailing attitude toward coercive and violent behavior such as bullying. I believe we must wake up to the fact that cynicism and indifference erode society at its roots and are potentially more dangerous than any individual act of evil.

Two men with whom I copublished a series of dialogues, the renowned Russian children's author Albert A. Likhanov and Norman Cousins, known as the "conscience of America," both shared this view. They adamantly warned against the dangers of indifference and cynicism in the face of evil — even more than evil itself — because these attitudes reveal a decisive lack of passionate engagement with life, an isolation and withdrawal from reality.

Citing the paradoxical words of Bruno Jasienski, Likhanov warns of the profound harm apathy inflicts on a young person's soul:

> Do not fear your enemies. The worst they can do is kill you. Do not fear friends. At worst, they may betray you. Fear those who do not care; they neither kill nor

betray, but betrayal and murder exist because of their silent consent.[4]

In other words, it is the act of averting our eyes from acts of murder or betrayal that allows such evil to proliferate without end. Similarly, Cousins makes reference to the following statement by Robert Louis Stevenson:

> I hate cynicism a great deal more than I do the devil, unless perhaps the two are the same thing.[5]

He voices his own deep concern that the defeatism and self-doubt characteristic of a pessimistic attitude will undermine and destroy such values as idealism, hope and trust.

A state of life controlled by apathy and cynicism grows immune to emotions of love or hatred, suffering or joy, and retreats into a barren, makeshift world of alienation. Indifference toward evil implies indifference toward good. It makes for a bleak state of life and a semantic space estranged from the vital drama of the struggle between good and evil.

Children's keen senses quickly detect the apathy and cynicism rampant in an adult world bereft of values. Perhaps for this reason, adults become uneasy when they see in children's hearts an eerie and familiar darkness.

Evil, like good, is an undeniable reality. Without evil there is no good, and without good there is no evil: they coexist and are defined by their complementarity. Depending on one's response or reaction, evil can be transformed to good or good to evil. In this sense, they are both relative and transmutable. We must therefore recognize that both good and evil are defined in relation to their opposite or "other," and that the "self" is defined by this dynamic.

"Self" in Absence of "Other"

In Buddhism, we find the concepts of the oneness of good and evil and the fundamental neutrality of life with regard to good and evil. As an example, for the historical Buddha Shakyamuni (representing good) to attain enlightenment and thereby fulfill his purpose in life there had to exist an opposing, evil "other," in this case his cousin Devadatta, who sought to undermine and then destroy him. In contrast, the failure to acknowledge and reconcile oneself with the existence of an opposing "other" is the basic flaw in an apathetic, cynical approach to life, in which only the isolated self exists.

A truer, fuller sense of self is found in the totality of the psyche that is inextricably linked to "other." Carl Jung distinguished between "Ego," which knows only the outer content of the psyche, and "Self," which knows its inner content as well and unifies the conscious and the unconscious. In the world of apathy and cynicism we find only an isolated sense of self roaming the superficies of the conscious mind — what Jung refers to as ego.

The "self" lacking identification with the "other" is insensitive to the pain, anguish and suffering of the "other." It tends to confine itself to its own world, either sensing threat in the slightest provocation and triggering violent behavior, or nonresponsively turning away in detachment.

I would venture to say this mentality provided the nesting ground of the fanatical ideologies, such as fascism and Bolshevism, which swept through the twentieth century. We have more recently witnessed the birth of virtual reality, which can also, I believe, further obscure the "other." Viewed in this light, it is clear that none of us can remain a mere spectator or view the problematic behavior of children as someone else's responsibility.

In the course of a discussion, peace scholar Johan Galtung mentioned to me that the prerequisite for an "outer dialogue" is an "inner dialogue."[6] If the concept of "other" is absent from "self," true dialogue cannot take place.

Exchanges between two individuals both lacking a sense of "other" might appear to be dialogue but are in fact simply the trading of one-sided statements. Communication inevitably fails. Most distressing in this kind of semantic space — at once voluble and empty — is that words lose their resonance and are eventually stifled and expire. The demise of words naturally means the demise of an essential aspect of our humanity — the capacity for language that earned us the name *Homo loquens* (speaking man).

Reality can be revealed only through genuine dialogue, where "self" and "other" transcend the narrow limits of ego and fully interact. This inclusive sense of reality expresses a human spirituality abounding in vitality and empathy.

In a lecture I gave at Harvard University in 1991, I stated that the times require an ethos of "soft power." I suggested that an inner-motivated spirituality constitutes the essence of soft power and that this derives from inner-directed processes. It becomes manifest when the soul has struggled through phases of suffering, conflict, ambivalence, mature deliberation and, finally, resolution.

It is only in the burning furnace of intense, soul-baring exchanges — the ceaseless and mutually supporting processes of inner and outer dialogue between one's "self" and a profoundly internalized "other" — that our beings are tempered and refined. Only then can we begin to grasp and fully affirm the reality of being alive. Only then can we bring forth the brilliance of a universal spirituality that embraces all humankind.

The Inner Realm of the Soul and Religious Sentiment

I believe that the spiritual heritage of humanity can be found in its great works of literature, which may be considered the quintessential representation of the inner self. Here, I would like to draw on *The House of the Dead*, a work said to have marked a turning point in Dostoevsky's career as a writer.

The young Dostoevsky was sentenced for allegedly harboring revolutionary ideas to four years of hard labor in the bitter cold of Siberia. *The House of the Dead* is unparalleled in documenting the common virtues of humankind revealed to him through this terrible ordeal.

> [T]he common people . . . never reproach a criminal with the crime that he has committed, whatever it may be. They forgive him in consideration of the sentence passed upon him.

> It is well known that the common people throughout Russia call crime a "misfortune," and the criminal an "unfortunate." This definition is expressive and profound, though unconscious and instinctive.[7]

The "unfortunate" — an unusual choice of words yet rich in significance. Perhaps it shows Dostoevsky's somewhat romantic view of the Russian people. Be that as it may, I trust the insight of a great writer who goes beyond the superficial to speak of the inner realm of the soul.

To call a crime a "misfortune" and a criminal an "unfortunate" reflects a breadth of perception inclusive of "other." No distinction is made between oneself and the criminal; the expression exudes a sense of empathetic connection.

When in the midst of adversity empathy remains high, a healthy flow of communication prevails. On the other hand, the loss of a sense of connection between people signals the breakdown of communication in a society. Unable to communicate, to recognize the worth of an individual life, people find themselves endlessly debating — and incapable of answering — the straightforward question: "Why is it wrong to kill?"

Thoughtless arrogance, the root of all ideological evil, presupposes that oneself is good and the "other" is evil. By contrast, the attitude described by Dostoevsky enables one to see that a person compelled by circumstances toward evil can also be inspired toward good. From this view emanates the expansive "inner impulse of compassion"[8] that Rousseau deemed the primordial foundation of society.

This natural compassion resonates closely with what Mahayana Buddhism terms the Bodhisattva Way, the epitome of which may be found in the words of Bodhisattva Vimalakirti — "Because all living beings are sick, therefore I am sick"[9] — and in the example of Jesus of Nazareth who focused more love and compassion on the one "stray sheep" than all the rest.

The running theme in Dostoevsky's later works is theodicy, a defense of God's justice in creating a world in which both good and evil exist. Central to Rousseau's thoughts on education is a religious sentiment independent of, and unbounded by, church dogma and authority. It would seem that at the heart of universal feelings of empathy and spirituality thrives some form of religious sentiment and that this is inherent in human beings.

In the twentieth century, a century of war and violence, we find also the bright light of spirituality emanating from the nonviolent struggles of Mahatma Gandhi and Martin Luther King, Jr. One might ask how their struggles became mass movements and why many people today embrace nonviolence. Like Gandhi, who asserted that religion "provides a moral basis to all other activities which they otherwise lack,"[10] I believe the answer lies beneath the words and actions of these leaders. They each based themselves on a strong religious conviction, which enabled them to remain unswayed by any adversity.

An Absence of Values

American psychologist Abraham H. Maslow offered an important insight into education from the perspective of spirituality.

According to Maslow, the primary consideration of education is to "help [the student] to become the best he is capable of becoming, to become actually what he deeply is potentially."[11] His view closely parallels Makiguchi's view that consistently placed the happiness of learners at the center of education.

Maslow insisted that we must never take our eyes off the "far goals" and "ultimate values" of education, lest we lose sight of the highest potential attainable by human beings and end up confusing our priorities.[12] Arguably Japan, with its current educational crisis, should find his warning disquieting. After all, it is a crisis brought on by decades of educational policies shaped by the perceived immediate needs of either the military or the economy.

To my view, the long-term values Maslow approached from philosophical, religious, humanistic and ethical angles equate with the cultivation of spirituality and broad religious sentiment.

In November 2000, I had the opportunity to meet with Victor Kazanjian, dean of religious and spiritual life at Wellesley College and one of the cofounders of The Education as Transformation Project. With some 350 participating colleges and universities across the United States, the project seeks to redress the current state of education in which ties between individuals and between individuals and society have eroded. It aims for the embrace of wholeness and spirituality in education.

Dean Kazanjian has noted the increasing dissociation between intellectual training and spiritual values, along with the growing trend that views education simply as a means or instrumentality. Consequently, he has expressed high hopes for Soka University of America's humanistic approach to education, which aims to nurture the whole individual. In fact, this aim is the heart and guiding ethic of Soka education that has been painstakingly developed since Makiguchi's time.

The turmoil in education and the consequent darkness enveloping the lives of children point to an eroded ability to educate on the part of society as a whole and its constituent elements — not only those institutions with formal responsibility for educational and religious matters but including the family and the community.

We cannot continue merely treating the symptoms of this malaise. I am not alone in believing we have reached the point at which we must opt for a comprehensive strategy. Maslow aptly raised the question of whether a "value-free education" is at all desirable. Perhaps it is time to choose a response that resonates with the spirituality and faith in the depths of the human heart.

Against Compulsory Religious Education in Japan

Here I wish to be very clear about this point. In no way am I proposing a return to formal, state-sanctioned religious education in Japan. To do so would be to ignore the painful lessons of pre-World War II Japan's enshrinement of State Shinto as the official religion of the nation. This had, of course, an overwhelming impact on schools at the time, turning them into a delivery system for force-feeding the population with militarism and nationalism. Both the postwar Japanese Constitution and the Fundamental Law of Education expressly prohibit religious education in public schools, and for good reason.

Lately we hear from certain quarters in Japanese society the resurgent strains of ultranationalism. These voices call for the reinstatement of religious education in public schools as a means to restore social discipline. I am adamantly opposed to repeating the tragic manipulation of young minds that took place in prewar Japan. I am absolutely against compulsory religious education that would trample on the freedoms of thought and religion.

The Soka Gakkai's commitment to human rights can be traced to the spiritual struggles waged by its first president, Tsunesaburo Makiguchi, and its second president, Josei Toda. Both men gave their all to combat the totalitarianism that robbed citizens of their spiritual freedom and mobilized the Japanese nation into war.

Freedom of religion, though guaranteed by the Japanese Constitution, cannot be taken for granted. For this reason I have made it a point to speak out in protest against religious education in public schools. The proposition infringes basic rights and runs counter to the Fundamental Law of Education, Article IX, which reads: "The schools established by the state and local public bodies shall refrain from religious education or activities for a specified religion."

Of course, private schools can provide religious education as it accords with their educational philosophies, goals and religious values. This is not a cause for concern as long as the children's personal freedom of religion is not infringed.

On this point, the Soka schools form part of a private educational system ranging from kindergarten to the university level, and they focus on value-creating education. Religious doctrine is not taught, nor is it incorporated into any class. With the aim of developing students' abilities to ponder meaning and purpose, the schools' mission is to foster a rich humanism and spirituality that will enable students to enjoy personal growth and contribute to society.

The Cultivation of Religious Sentiment

How to inspire spirituality and religious sentiment is a challenge that has exercised humanity throughout history. I maintain that if we are to revive in education its ability to foster spirituality and broad religious sentiment, every individual, every family, every organization and every sector of society must pool their energies and resources.

In other words, the role of religion is inseparable from the individual and society: Religion must enable individuals to achieve their personal goals as well as contribute positively to society. Were these intertwining paths to diverge, religious sentiment would be reduced to sectarianism; religion would degenerate into something antihumanistic and antisocial. Any religious movement that considers its role and mission as separate from society is, in my view, making a fundamental error. There is a sharp distinction between the broad religious sentiment I describe here and narrow sectarianism.

Any religious sentiment that does not enable individuals to create value or take constructive action in their personal lives and in society is deceptive and does not deserve to be called religious at all.

Whether a religion can move beyond sectarianism and whether the spirituality and religious sentiment it inspires can garner universal understanding will be the test of that faith tradition's ability to contribute to civilization in the twenty-first century. This is the reason I must state once more my grave concerns regarding the dangers of reintroducing sectarian religious education into public schools.

Building Character through Reading

I believe that the means to encourage a flowering in the neglected inner lives of children will always be exposure to literature and the arts. In short, I believe the key is to be found in reading books.

The first step in reviving dialogue where human bonds and communication have broken down is to revitalize and infuse the written and spoken word with the light of spirituality. Literary masterpieces are the ideal vehicle for this endeavor, which should not be limited to schools. From my own experience, I can say that the experience of immersing oneself in the world's greatest literature at a young age is an invaluable, lifelong asset.

In Japan, the school system affords children various opportunities to read literature. In many cases, however, these works are delivered in the form of Japanese-language textbooks designed mainly to improve reading skills. More reading programs are now being instituted in schools across Japan, but perhaps the aim should be higher: Serious consideration should also be given to making world literature a core subject in the school curriculum.

In the Swedish school system, the educational curriculum is designed to reflect no bias in favor of any specific religion. Student motivation and initiative to read are central to the educational program, in that students are given the freedom to select topics of interest from a broad range of texts. Encouraging the children in this way hones their powers of insight and reasoning, so they are equipped to grapple with the fundamental and ethical issues facing modern civilization. Surely, as Japan reexamines educational methods and their implementation, it can benefit greatly from the examples of other countries.

In a sense, reading presents a summation of the author's life experiences. In *Nagai saka* (The Long Slope), popular novelist Shugoro Yamamoto notes:

> Life is long. Whether one reaches the summit in one bound or steadily scales the mountain step by step, the destination is the same. Rather than accomplishing the journey in one bound, scaling the mountain step by step affords one the opportunity to enjoy the scenery along the way. The trees. The plants. The springs. Moreover, one can have confidence in knowing that each step has been taken carefully and securely. This becomes the source of greater strength.[13]

His imaginative and profound words can be applied easily to the experience of reading. Reading the classics is challenging.

Even when they are not lengthy, grasping their essence is not as easy as it is for, say, comic books. A complex passage may require rereading two or three times before it makes some kind of sense. Some passages may defy immediate comprehension, requiring instead the light of time.

Certainly, these arduous efforts are much like those of a mountain climber who carefully checks for secure footing and remains alert to his surroundings as he makes his way to the summit. Reading digests or synopses of great works does them no justice. Only when we have painstakingly struggled to grasp the full meaning of a book does it become part of our flesh and blood.

While reading alone at one's desk has its merits, the value of the reading experience is augmented when shared with friends or teachers. It is heightened by the exchange of ideas, especially when one considers reading a lifelong habit. My own teenage years, spent amidst the burnt rubble of the postwar period, were enriched immeasurably by a reading circle formed with the youth in my neighborhood. Also forever etched in my life are precious memories of reading sessions with my mentor, Josei Toda.

My mentor never tired of encouraging us to be active, never passive, readers; to strive to absorb but not be overwhelmed by books. A master of life, he taught me through his attitude and words this invaluable lesson: The way we relate to books is the way we relate to people, and encountering a good book is the same as encountering a good mentor or a good friend.

The Dangers of Virtual Reality

I have a second reason for insisting on the importance of reading. An accumulation of experience in reading can act as a buffer to shield one's inner life from the adverse influences of what is popularly termed *virtual reality*.

Clearly, the projection of images in virtual reality has some utilitarian value. But it is also true that it distorts as well as simulates real-life experiences in which people share an empathic resonance through direct contact with one another and with nature. On the purely harmful side, the overpowering stimulation and excitement that virtual reality produces can lull the imagination and numb sympathetic feelings for real pain and suffering.

Once inured to the conditioning of virtual reality, people may turn into mere passive receptors of programmed images. Active faculties, components of an inner-motivated spirituality — the powers, for example, to think critically, to make decisions, to love and sympathize, to stand against evil, to believe — tend to atrophy.

Scientist and philosopher Albert Jacquard has made the following observation:

> Information science, inasmuch as it provides information, is valuable. However, it supplies only communication canned or frozen. It is incapable of evoking the bursts of creativity that come naturally in the course of a dialogue comprising moments of silence as well as words.[14]

His way of describing dehumanized communication is very apt. Reading, on the other hand, generates a restorative breeze of inspiration in the depths of one's soul — a capacity well beyond that of such "frozen" communication. After all, the experience of reading comes down to a tenacious, intimate dialogue between author and reader. This is the reason I refer to the world of reading as a rich summation of life experiences.

Yet another reason to value reading is that it affords youth and adults alike the opportunity to rise above the routine experiences of everyday life and ponder their past and future prospects. Be it from a book previously read or one pored over for the first time, we feel something genuine, we are moved as every fiber of our being grapples with its content. Without such full engagement, it would be nearly impossible to share our impressions of books with children. The truth resonates with the listener not through empty words but through the richness and depth of one's own character.

Above all else, the experience of reading nurtures the spontaneity of children's curiosity. It encourages their self-discipline to take time for reflection and develops their capacity to seek solutions from within.

Tolstoy's Portrait of Spiritual Transformation

World literature is a treasure house of questions, of reflection and wonderment.

Let us draw from a scene in the final chapter of Tolstoy's *Anna Karenina*, where the protagonist Levin asks himself, "What am I? And where am I? And why am I here?"[15]

Levin, said to portray Tolstoy himself, is seeking the reason for his existence when he encounters a peasant whose words transform him. Tolstoy deftly and poignantly captures this transformation, the opening of new horizons and the subsequent opening and flowering of Levin's emotions.

> Well, that's how it is — people are different. One man just lives for his own needs, take Mityukha even, just stuffs his belly, but Fokanych — he's an upright old man. He lives for the soul. He remembers God.[16]

To live for one's soul — these simple words, spoken nonchalantly by a peasant, pierce Levin's heart. Walking along the road, he continues his soliloquy as he savors this novel sensation.

> He felt something new in his soul and delightedly probed this new thing, not yet knowing what it was.[17]

As he finally becomes satisfied that he has gleaned the answer, Levin turns into the woods to lie down on the grass and thinks to himself:

> I haven't discovered anything. I've only found out what I know. I've understood that power which not only gave me life in the past but is giving me life now. I am freed from deception, I have found the master.[18]

Images of transformation from darkness to light appear frequently in Tolstoy's works: typically from questioning to effusive inspiration from the contact of two souls; then through self-examination to the discovery and formation of a new self. These processes truly capture the workings of the spirit.

By virtue of his vital spirituality regained, Levin sees through the deception of war to its harsh and simple reality — human beings killing one another. The dawning truth seeps into his interjection: "'But it's not just to sacrifice themselves, it's also to kill Turks.'"[19] His observation casts doubt on the legitimacy of the nationalistic fervor that made self-sacrifice in the Serbian War a noble undertaking. The eternal commandment "Thou shalt not kill" gains new meaning and is imbued with a sense of immediacy when invoked by one like Levin who has lived through spiritual agony and torment.

What I regard as the climactic point of the story appears in the closing scene, where Levin bares his doubts:

> As he was going into the nursery, he remembered what he had hidden from himself. It was that if the main proof of the Deity is His revelation of what is good, then why was this revelation limited to the Christian Church alone?[20]
>
> Well, but the Jews, the Mohammedans, the Confucians, the Buddhists — what are they? . . . Can these hundreds of millions of people be deprived of the highest good, without which life has no meaning?[21]

I regard Tolstoy's *Anna Karenina* as unparalleled in its portrayal of the spirituality and religious sentiment residing in every human soul.

Enrichment Through Reading

The extent to which serious reading and appreciation of literature can enrich and create substance in our inner world defies description. Allowing our common spiritual heritage to go to waste would be a source of deep regret.

This is true not only of Tolstoy's works. The same can be said of books by Dostoevsky, Hugo and Goethe, among many others. For decades, even centuries, these classics have ranked highly among a myriad of works. Surely they are replete with substance. For anyone who finds world literature daunting, there are modern classics in one's own language and children's books such as those recommended by the Jungian psychologist Hayao Kawai in Japan. The choices are endless.

There are those who would say we have become distant from the printed word. I share this concern, and it is for just this reason that I wish to extol the value of reading in one's youth. It is truly sad to find young people who have not experienced the thrilling challenge of mastering even one literary classic. It is my abiding hope that preschoolers and schoolchildren be afforded every opportunity to be exposed to reading at home as well as in school. While there is much children gain from reading on their own, the experience is further enriched when parents and teachers read aloud to them.

Children sense the warmth of words in the voices of their parents and teachers, and their imagination is challenged to capture a story's landscapes and dramatic scenes. The modulations of the reader's voice help children experience and develop a range of emotions, from sadness to joy. As parents and teachers read aloud, they can watch the children's facial expressions and choose to change their tone or pause to hear a child's thoughts. Through these encounters, a relationship of mutual trust steadily begins to take shape.

Just as a farmer sows seeds and prays for a bountiful crop, it is important for adults to read to children in the hope that they will grow up healthy and strong, limitlessly develop their potential, and realize every dream. Every facet of a child's development depends on that child's reassurance and confidence that someone believes in him or her, that someone cares.

Education and the Future

On a final note, I believe some programs sponsored by the educators division of the Soka Gakkai offer one example of reinforcing society's ability to educate.

By way of introduction, in 1968, members of the educators division, determined to contribute to their local community, launched an Educational Counseling Program. In the thirty-two years of its existence, this program has provided volunteer educational counseling services to some 280,000 people. At present, eight hundred members of the educators division are active as counselors in twenty-eight communities throughout Japan. All are current or retired teachers who have acquired a background in educational counseling. On a weekly basis, they provide counseling to those who are experiencing difficulties within the educational system, reinforcing their skills through peer review of case studies. The program is open to all members of the community, without regard to religious affiliation, and all advice and counseling are given purely from a secular educational perspective.

A further program was launched in 1999 in an effort to support education in the family and the community. A designated senior educational counselor serves as a liaison with the local community, organizing informal discussions on educational issues. Eventually this system will be expanded to reach communities throughout Japan.

Due to the steady efforts of the committed individuals involved in this counseling, there are numerous stories of children who have regained their confidence and made a fresh start. To help a suffering child or parent who is feeling isolated because of various difficulties, I believe it is necessary to supplement the counseling provided by schools and by the government. Educational counseling incorporated into community services would make access to professional help easier and less intimidating. In other words, society must draw on collective efforts to help overcome the current problems in education.

According to their records, absenteeism or refusal to attend school now accounts for 70 percent of the cases brought to the Educational Counseling Program. In almost half of these cases, fear of bullying is the reason children feel unable or unwilling to go to school.

In the face of these realities, we cannot remain idle. Our whole society must show a greater concern if we are to counter the problems of bullying and other acts of violence. We are in urgent need of a social ethos that will not accept or condone violence in any form. We must reverse the tide of indifference and cynicism now permeating society.

A strengthened capacity to educate, the weaving of education into every thread of our social fabric, the permeation of a sense of commitment and a responsibility to educate — such concrete developments, and not simply politics or the economy, are what will determine the future. Our children's happiness rests in the balance. Qualified only by an overarching commitment to establish this century as the century of education, it is my earnest desire to work together with like-minded people around the world to continually swell the tide of humanistic education.

3

Serving the Essential Needs of Education

September 29, 2000

Education in Crisis

As we enter the twenty-first century, education is once again the focus of considerable discussion. In Japan, this debate has concentrated on educational reform. I would like to respond to recent points raised and offer some frank opinions on this debate as well as make some concrete proposals.

One widespread problem recently has been that of children who, for various reasons, particularly bullying, refuse to attend school. It is said this problem could affect almost any child in Japan: The Ministry of Education's annual survey of Japanese schools has revealed that absenteeism in elementary and junior high schools reached an unprecedented 130,000-plus students in 1999. This means that, at the elementary-school level, one out of every 290 students is unable or unwilling to attend school and, at the junior-high level, one out of forty, an average of one student in every class.

In Japan, there has been a terrible series of school-age suicides and other tragedies resulting from bullying, and the crisis is escalating, while the worldwide problem of drug abuse is gradually spreading to Japan as well. In addition, a succession of juvenile crimes in recent years has shocked the Japanese public: a series of murders by fourteen- and fifteen-year-olds; the motiveless expressway bus hijacking by a seventeen-year-old, killing one and causing severe traumas for all other passengers; and a mother brutally clubbed to death with a baseball bat by her son. Crimes such as these would have been practically unthinkable in Japan just a few years ago.

Professionals in the fields of juvenile psychology and education analyze these issues, looking for solutions. Realistically speaking, however, adult society has still failed to deal successfully with these problems. Shocked at their monstrosity, we feel helpless in the face of these unfathomable trends.

As one individual who aspires to promote the sound growth of the young people who are to shoulder our future, I penned a proposal in 1984 for a general meeting of the Soka Gakkai's nationwide education division (see page 161). Based on the principle that educational reform should be driven by humanism, not politics, I indicated in that proposal a humanistic ideal imbued with creativity, internationalism and totality.

I recall that at that time, too, education was a major concern, and parents and teachers and many other interested individuals were deeply worried about the issues of problematic behavior, school violence and absenteeism. Since then, sadly, notwithstanding the efforts of those involved, not only has there been no improvement, but this situation has now become the norm and numerous new problems have subsequently emerged.

The Flight From Learning

One of the most serious problems recently has been the breakdown of discipline in schools as classes become uncontrollable due to students' disruptive behavior. This problem was initially marked at the junior high school level but has been affecting even the elementary school level in recent years. In the worst cases, children resist attempts at discipline already by the time they enter elementary school, totally disrupting classes.

Surveys show that a third of the homeroom teachers responsible for these children are so frustrated that they have considered giving up altogether. If nothing is done, we may see the breakdown of the entire school system.

Another acute problem is a decline in academic achievement. Students' aversion to study, as seen in their dislike of subjects such as mathematics and science, is becoming a serious problem. Various studies demonstrate how the academic level of Japanese children is deteriorating altogether and that this is now affecting high school and further education. There are reports, which would almost be laughable if they were not so shocking, of university students who lack a grasp of even the most basic concepts.

I would refer to this situation as a "flight from learning." I don't think it would be overdramatic to describe this trend as the defeat of education, the failure of our education system to fulfill its essential functions: the provision of spiritual nourishment, which enables us to develop our creativity through learning from the wisdom of our predecessors and thus gain access to the common cultural assets that humankind conveys from generation to generation.

In 2002, Japan will complete the phased reduction of the school week to five days from the traditional six. In tandem with this, the Ministry of Education has introduced a revised curriculum aiming to cultivate children's "zest for living" by providing latitude for their growth. This move must, I think, reflect criticism of the conventional cramming method that places too much emphasis on rote learning and furious examination competition and is among the principal causes of the "flight from learning."

There are many doubts, however, as to whether this change will lead to a genuine revival of learning or a comprehensive improvement of academic ability among students. These concerns are based on the possibility that if the number of classroom hours is reduced as proposed, rather than promoting voluntary study as intended, the extra hours will most probably result in children either spending more time in cramming schools or more hours watching television and playing video games and so not necessarily produce the expected results.

I share these anxieties. Although the suffering of children, as reflected by absenteeism, must be tackled immediately, I cannot possibly believe that the underlying problems can be fixed just by tinkering with the system.

Children Are the Mirror of Society

So what is behind our children's pathology of staying away from school, problematic behavior and the "flight from learning," which is rampant in contemporary society? I believe the fundamental cause is the overall decline of the educational functions that should be inherent not only in schools but in our communities, families and society as a whole.

If education, in the widest sense, enables human beings to truly express their humanity, then there must be a functional disorder in contemporary Japanese society that prevents individuals from becoming genuinely mature. This breakdown is manifested most acutely in the most fragile and sensitive constituent of our society, that is, the children. At the risk of oversimplification, we must never forget the time-honored saying "Children are the mirror of society" when considering the problems of education.

Unless adults possess a kind of self-reflective attitude to correct in themselves that which is mirrored back to them by their children, attempts to reform the system, however well intentioned, may ultimately end up as stopgap or temporary measures that merely work around the edges of the system.

I found the following words in an article on moral education by the writer Taichi Yamada very moving: "Our children need more than empty sermons about virtue. As adults, we must somehow demonstrate to them in practice how to live a better life."[1]

The truth is, however, that the adult world suddenly revealed after Japan's rapid economic growth and in the aftermath of the "bubble" economy collapse is in an extremely wretched and gloomy state, approaching the new century with practically no vitality. Be it in politics, the bureaucracy, business or the media, the elite have behaved shamefully, totally bent on vindicating themselves, evading social responsibility and protecting their own interests.

Japanese society is rife with materialism and scandalous corruption among adults, a situation indicated by a spate of insurance-related murder cases that demonstrate our loss of values and sense of purpose. This has definitely cast a dark shadow in the hearts of our children. In a society lacking role models who can inspire the next generation, of course education cannot function properly.

Doubtless, large numbers of individuals are unaffected by the sensationalism of the media and continue to work sincerely. They adhere to a belief that what is essential is, in Mr. Yamada's words, to "demonstrate in practice how to live a better life." Even these people, however, are finding it difficult to uphold their principles. The fact that people increasingly extol an over-idealized image of "the good old days of the Meiji era"[2] perhaps reflects that people feel a spiritual deficiency in contemporary Japanese society.

Review of the Fundamental Law of Education

I believe these problems are also part of the reason behind calls for a review and possible amendment of the Fundamental Law of Education, the mainstay of the postwar education system, as part of a series of educational reform plans.

The July 2000 report by the prime minister's private advisory board, the National Council on Educational Reform, stated that the majority view was that an amendment of the Fundamental Law of Education was required, and that "in the preamble and provisions in Article 1, there is an overemphasis on individual and universal humanity and an omission of respect toward the nation, the community, tradition, culture, the home, and nature."

In fact, it is hard to find fault with the principles stated in the preamble or in Article 1, which stipulates the objectives of education as follows:

> Education shall aim at the full development of personality, striving for the rearing of the people, sound in mind and body, who shall love truth and justice, esteem individual value, respect labor and have a deep sense of responsibility, and be imbued with the independent spirit, as builders of the peaceful state and society.[3]

This is a perfectly acceptable statement of the universal principle of "full development of personality" based on respect for individual dignity, and it is pertinent to peoples of all times and cultures.

In applying this universal principle, however, its relevance must be tested in the social and ethical context. I feel in this sense that those who drafted this law were not specific enough. People failed to delve into what the individual, in this context, really means. In fact, the individual can only become fully realized through interaction with others. In order to do this, it is necessary to control egoism. This is perhaps so self-evident that the drafters of the law failed to pay enough attention to it. They failed to be adequately aware of the dangers of individualism degenerating into selfish egoism.

Thus, any review or revision of the law proposed by the NCER must be based on a clear understanding of the way in which universal principles find expression within cultural particularities. And I believe that this same concern motivated Tatsuo Morito, the minister of education instrumental in drafting the Fundamental Law of Education, who later expressed doubts about its effectiveness.

Although not mentioned in the council's report, there is a reactionary mood in the country calling for a return to the spirit of the following section of the Imperial Rescript on Education to correct these deficiencies.

> Ye, Our subjects, be filial to your parents, affectionate to your brothers and sisters; as husbands and wives be harmonious, as friends true; bear yourselves in modesty and moderation; extend your benevolence to all. . . . [4]

Merely filling the text with references to culture, tradition and the home will not, I think, produce much effect. Without question, reinstatement of the virtues extolled in the Imperial Rescript on Education would be totally anachronistic when one considers the role the Rescript assumed in Japan's imperial and patriarchal systems before and during the war. Glorifying the values of loyalty and filial piety, the Imperial Rescript on Education was used as an absolute guiding principle of education and served as a powerful tool of ideological indoctrination.

The Fundamental Law of Education has been the mainstay of the postwar education system in Japan, and for this reason I believe any revision should be undertaken only after careful thought and review; hasty revision is to be avoided.

A Paradigm Shift

The modern Japanese educational system has reached a critical juncture. We are witnessing the consequences of making education subordinate to bureaucratic and political agendas under the control of the Ministry of Education.

Modern Japan's progress, whether it be the prewar policy of building national prosperity and military strength or the postwar stress on becoming an economic superpower, has been motivated by an unconditional national imperative to catch up with and surpass the West. At the same time, ever since the Meiji era, education has been coercively positioned as a means to attain these goals. Both of these approaches are now evidently at a stalemate as Japan is compelled to make an orbital change in direction from industrialization to adaptation to the information-oriented era.

Hence, as I consider education in the twenty-first century, I would like to assert that what is most urgently needed is a paradigm shift from looking at education for society's sake to building a society that serves the essential needs of education.

In formulating the conceptual paradigm of "a society that

serves the essential needs of education," I was inspired by Professor Robert Thurman of Columbia University. Each time I have had the chance to meet with him, I have been impressed by the depth of his vision. In an interview with the Boston Research Center for the 21st Century, he was asked how he viewed the role of education in society. He replied: "I think the question should rather be: What is the role of society in education? Because in my view education is the purpose of human life."

This is indeed a penetrating insight. Professor Thurman says that this view is largely due to influences from the teachings of Shakyamuni, whom he considers one of humanity's first teachers. This resonates with Kant's ethical philosophy, which insists that we respect the autonomy of others and that humans must never be used as a means to an end.

Learning is the very purpose of human life, the primary factor in the development of personality, that which makes human beings truly human. Nevertheless, development of personality has consistently been reduced to a subordinate position and viewed as a means to other ends. This view has prevailed worldwide throughout modern history, particularly in the twentieth century.

The educational system has therefore been reduced to a mere mechanism that serves national objectives, be they political, military, economic or ideological. A certain type of personality, not the full development of personality, has been sought, as if casting individuals from a uniform mold. Treating education as a means rather than an end reinforces a utilitarian view of human life itself.

It is a terrible tragedy that the twentieth century suffered ceaseless wars and violence and became an unprecedented era of mass killing. Needless to say, this demonstrates an increase in killing power, the negative legacy of technological advance. Furthermore, I feel that it is in large part due to an overturning of values in modern civilization, caused by ceasing to regard human beings as the basis of value and instead assigning merely subordinate roles to education, which should be a fundamental and primary human activity.

In this regard, I feel some anxiety about attitudes toward the IT revolution. As was described in the Okinawa Charter on Global Information Society at the Okinawa–Kyushu Summit this year, "Information and Communication Technology (IT) is one of the most potent forces in shaping the twenty-first century."[5] There can be no doubt that the IT revolution will become one of the mega-trends in the forthcoming century, and it is of course important not to be left behind.

University professors and officials have frequently noted that the deterioration of academic ability among Japanese students, especially in mathematics and sciences, if left unsolved, may negatively affect Japan's economy and technological ability and consequently delay Japan in the worldwide race toward the IT revolution. It is only right to be apprehensive in this regard.

While globalization naturally entails both positive and negative aspects, the current toward internationalization in the twenty-first century will be unstoppable. No country can remain unaffected.

Yet, my personal uneasiness is about the possibility of retracing the footsteps of the past, that is, returning to the idea of education for society's sake in tackling the problem of how to improve the academic level of our students.

Insofar as the IT revolution by nature has the potential to cause a paradigm shift in contemporary society, its influence contains positive and negative potentials. My observation of the current state of affairs, however, is that only the optimistic and positive aspects have been stressed.

In the United States — which anticipated the IT revolution first, especially in the financial sector, and sometimes appears to have carved out for itself a monopoly where materialism and "casino capitalism" thrive — the darkness of the IT revolution undoubtedly casts a growing shadow. If all that the new invention of IT brings to human society is a tendency toward materialism, then what use is this revolution?

A Society That Confuses Happiness With Pleasure

In the face of this tendency, we need to return to the core issue of human values. I believe we need to redefine the crucial concept of "development of personality."

People have come to take this phrase, described as the purpose of education in the Fundamental Law of Education, for granted. But this is a universal goal we must strive to realize and implement. It is a fundamental concept, and it can never be emphasized enough as the key to educational reform.

For this purpose, let us experiment by replacing the phrase *development of personality* with the word *happiness*. The first president of the Soka Gakkai, Tsunesaburo Makiguchi, an outstanding educator, never ceased to stress that the purpose of education is ensuring children's happiness.

Makiguchi's pedagogy is gradually gaining international recognition today, but it was originally conceived under Japan's prewar militarist regime, which mobilized every educational institution to foster obedient imperial subjects. Makiguchi protested against this process, asserting that education's true aim should be the lifelong well-being of children and critiquing the Imperial Rescript on Education as providing nothing more than a "minimum set of moral standards."

In other words, he was a farsighted individual who, during a period of fanatical militarism, held fast to his belief that society should serve the authentic needs of humanistic education and that education must never be sacrificed to nationalist goals.

Happiness, however, must not be confused with mere pleasure. Mistaking momentary pleasure for a life of genuine satisfaction and happiness exemplifies the skewing of values that in my opinion has been at the root of the distortions of postwar Japanese society. This mistaken attitude results in liberty yielding to indulgence and self-seeking, peace yielding to cowardice and indolence, human rights to complacency, and democracy to mobocracy.

Consequently, development of personality ceases, and we are left with immature and arrogant individuals, unable to grow out of their childish ways or listen to others, as described by José Ortega y Gasset.[6]

The experience of a truly human life — genuine happiness

— can only be realized in the bonds and interactions between people. Herein lies the essence of the Buddhist perspective on human life and happiness. Enmity, contradiction and discord may seem unavoidable aspects of relations among humans and our relations with nature and the universe. But, by persevering in spite of these conflicts, transforming them and restoring and rejuvenating the bonds among us, we can forge and polish our individuality and character.

If these bonds are severed, the human spirit can only roam aimlessly in the pitch darkness of solitude. In psychological terms this might be referred to as a "communication disorder," a pathology of modern society due to a weakening of the bonds among people.

Antisocial behavior and the increasing viciousness of juvenile crimes are acute manifestations of this social pathology. There is an ongoing debate in Japan about amending the juvenile law, but changing the law will not of itself lead to a solution. It is the responsibility of adults to patiently restore the ability to communicate by listening to the voices of isolated children calling out for help from the darkness.

There is a famous episode involving Socrates in which his influence on youth is described as being like an electric ray that stings those who touch it. He explains that he can electrify others because he is electrified himself. Similarly, teachers must constantly be creative if they are to evoke creativity in their students. This is an essential quality for educators.

Most important is the teacher's attitude. Human interaction is the key.

Restoring Human Bonds

Creative coexistence is clearly a key concept for the twenty-first century.

Communication between humans and the natural environment is also vital. In this respect also, Makiguchi had piercing foresight. At the opening of his book *The Geography of Human Life*,[7] Makiguchi stresses the importance of the influence of the natural environment on the development of personality by citing a work by the renowned educator and reformist Yoshida Shoin: "People do not develop in isolation from their environment, and human affairs are just a reflection of the people. Therefore, to understand human affairs, you first must understand the local context in which the people have developed." Makiguchi went on to state that you can only foster qualities of compassion, goodwill, friendship, kindness, sincerity and honesty, and cultivate nobility of the heart, within the local community.

The Geography of Human Life was published in 1903, more than half a century before environmental issues such as shortages of natural resources and energy and pollution of the atmosphere and water compelled humanity to reconsider its relationship with nature. Even then, Makiguchi keenly perceived that a breakdown of communication with nature not only causes humans physical damage but also results in the destruction of virtues such as compassion that are essential to the development of personality.

If the twentieth century was one in which human beings violently destroyed the global environment like rapacious invaders, then maintaining communication and contact with nature are absolutely indispensable in the education of our children and the young people who are to take responsibility for the twenty-first century. Just as with communication among humans, we must increase our opportunities to interact directly with nature rather than with the world of virtual reality. What can virtual reality offer to compare with the real-life sensation of communicating with nature — breathing the same air and basking in the same sunlight as the earth, trees, grass and animals — the dynamic expanse of life?

I recall a moving passage from an essay by Nobukiyo Takahashi, an authority on forest research.

> The beauty of the evening forest, especially under a full moon, throws into sharp contrast the boundary between the sky and the mountain ridges, as if viewing a wood-block print. It is a world of white and black. It is also a world savored only by those who experience it. Captured in photos or video, you may be able to discern these images to a certain extent, but you can never feel them in the same way. Because when you are there, it is not only through your eyes that you are touched: your skin senses the temperature and humidity; you smell the evening forest; fleetingly heard sounds that defy definition flit past your ears. Go out into the night forest, pick up a leaf, examine it front and back. How much beauty you can discover![8]

If we are to build a society that serves the essential needs of education in the twenty-first century, we must not become divided or isolated. Rather, we must deepen human bonds that transcend differences of race and nationality and also be in free and full communication with nature. We must give the highest priority to cultivating in young people the strength of character and values that will enable them to take the lead in building a world of creative coexistence.

The Independence of Education

Next, I would like to raise a few specific suggestions regarding reform of the education system.

Faced with the crisis in education, the National Council on Educational Reform was established in March 2000 as the Japanese prime minister's advisory board to discuss the direction of educational reform together with various Ministry of Education bodies.

While it is natural that education be recognized as a matter of utmost national importance, reform must not be conducted piecemeal by merely looking for remedies for specific problems but should be carried out with a long-term perspective. Since education is inextricably interrelated with society, the process of responding to changing times naturally may entail a degree of trial and error. Frequently, however, the orientation of reform has been strongly affected by the political current of the time or has consisted of myopic countermeasures that are simply reactions to changes in the immediate environment.

This was a problem in prewar Japan, as well. In *The System of Value-Creating Pedagogy*,[9] published seventy years ago, Makiguchi indicated: "As is the difficulty with any old, long-established edifice, our thoroughly inconsistent educational system has been patched up with an endless succession of stopgap remedial measures. Our schools are unable to respond to the demands of the new era and, as a result, are misdirecting the future progress of the young people who enter them. This is a truly distressing situation."

Challenging the myopic and superficial nature of contemporary Japanese attempts at educational reform, he proposed that two new institutions be established to develop an educational vision for a new era, namely, an "educational headquarters" to act as an independent, permanent central agency for education and a "national institute for educational research" to assist it. The latter was indeed founded soon after the war, but a central agency as he envisaged it has yet to be realized.

The NCER could potentially fulfill this function, but as this is an ad hoc body, there is the risk that this important issue might be treated in a stopgap way. This is why I propose the establishment of a permanent central commission for education committed to the long-term reconstruction of the entire framework of the educational system. This should be launched as an independent body institutionally insulated from all political influence. Ensuring independence is indispensable as a means to prevent a loss of continuity in educational policies in the event of changes in the administration and also to avoid arbitrary reforms caused by political interference.

I have in the past called for the principle of the separation of powers to be expanded to give education a status and independence equal to that accorded the executive, legislative and judicial branches of government. Because education is a profound endeavor that shapes the individuals of future generations, it should be completely independent of political interference. This also was the spirit of Makiguchi and his close associate and successor, Josei Toda, who both campaigned selflessly during the 1920s and 1930s against the nationalistic education pushing Japan on the path toward war.

Such a permanent central commission should then take the lead in setting forth firm principles and long-term directions for reform in education while communicating with organizations such as the National Institute for Educational Research of Japan.

In addition to this vital mission, this permanent central commission would have a broader focus that could enable Japan to open a new path toward international contribution. International exchange and cooperation in the educational arena, transcending national interests, will serve as a foundation for world peace. For this reason I have been promoting a vision, conceived more than twenty years ago, for what might be called a "United Nations of Education"[10] to work toward making education independent of political interference throughout the world.

If Japan could take on the role of promoting the independence of education throughout the world by establishing a permanent educational commission in this way, this would doubtless help create a new identity for Japan as a country devoted to education.

In April 2000, Japan sponsored the first G8 Education Summit, attended by education ministers. I propose that Japan actively support the regular holding of future international educational summits, promoting a broad range of exchanges not only at the governmental level but also among individuals actually engaged in education. As confirmed at the G8 Education Summit, educational issues are not limited to individual countries. Hence Japan should assume a pivotal role in leading other countries toward international cooperation to open a new horizon for education in the twenty-first century.

Balanced Reform

Next, here are some points pertaining to reform of education in schools, which has recently become a focal issue in Japan.

The core of this reform has been structural deregulation. The intention is that liberalization in the field of education will be promoted by abolishing the exams between junior and senior high schools in the public school system and introducing greater choice of schools. The reforms also include a reduction in overall class hours, aiming to provide more latitude for children's growth by introducing a five-day school week. These measures are presumably a result of recognizing the importance of encouraging competition among schools and in reaction against rote learning.

In the Japanese context, if these reforms are enacted without completely thinking them through and providing the resources to ensure they work, we may end up asking too much of children's self-motivation. Makiguchi described the impact that the indiscriminate advocacy of "freedom" can have on the educational process: "Mere liberation, unaccompanied by a creative, constructive element, falls into directionless indulgence. When one thinks of the impact on the educational economy of the innocent pupils, it is impossible to regard this with indifference."[11]

This warning from the past should not be neglected today. Our communities, schools and families need thorough, prudent preparation. As Makiguchi emphasized, methodological reforms must be preceded by unambiguously defining the purpose of education in terms of the happiness of students. Institutional changes not guided by clearly defined goals and principles could easily backfire as they have done in the past.

Makiguchi proposed a half-day school system, and of course this would reduce the amount of time spent at school, but he was not motivated merely by opposition to an overemphasis of rote learning as is the case at present. His intention was to achieve spiritually and physically balanced growth, whereby children could experience simultaneously the enrichment derived from learning at school and that derived from practical experience in society.

Makiguchi stressed: "The malady of contemporary education is not so much that there is an overemphasis on factual knowledge, but that educators' approach to the concept of intellectual education is not appropriate."[12] He called for a comprehensive change in Japanese attitudes toward education, shifting from an emphasis on factual knowledge alone to the development of intellect and wisdom. He felt this challenge should be addressed by schools.

Rather than focusing critically on the existing school system, curtailing its functions so as to attack its very foundations, I believe we should seek reform toward restoring our schools' fundamental function as the forum for imparting intellectual education in the true sense of the phrase.

Creativity and Experimentation

If we are to truly change school education, empowerment of teachers must be a component. I propose a transition to a more decentralized approach, which gives each school a freer hand and gives more authority to principals through democratization and transparency in the appointment process as well as encouraging the creativity and ingenuity of teachers. Because reforms have in the past been imposed uniformly, I believe it has been difficult for teachers to formulate new ideas as various restrictions lead them merely to perform their part adequately and no more.

Education should be for the sake of children and should not be under the monopolistic control of the government. In Japan, the government is deeply involved with details such as screening of textbooks and imposition of the curriculum, which means we have not cultivated the means to nurture autonomy of schools and teachers or the individuality and creativity of children.

Uniform standards should be limited to matters of basic framework, and the independence of the school should be respected in practical matters. At the same time, teachers should encourage one another to enhance the quality of education through trial and error.

In recent discussions on reform, there has been an ongoing debate about the quality of individual teachers, including suggestions that teaching certificates be subject to periodic renewal. What is really needed, however, is for the entire school to unite behind the challenge of enhancing the quality of education across the board. An example of this might be to have all teachers regularly open their classes to observation by their peers, as well as promoting exchanges among teachers of other subjects and from other neighborhood schools for the purpose of research.

The traditional Japanese system is reaching its limits, as seen in the breakdown of the lifetime employment and promotion by seniority systems in our companies. Positive competition is required if we are to reinvigorate our society. To enrich school education, teachers need mutual inspiration and motivation, encouragement and solidarity. Moreover, regular open days for children's families and members of the community as well as exchanges of views among elementary, junior and senior high school teachers in the same community would be useful in deepening cooperation.

In this context, I propose that new and different types of schools be officially accredited and experimental classes be promoted — a shift to decentralization for the genuine, internal transformation of school education in Japan through encouraging the creative energy of educators.

Other countries recognize a variety of schools operating under differing educational approaches — the Steiner schools grounded in a unique educational philosophy, the charter schools in the United States and "free schools" that enable children to select their own subjects of interest. Japan needs a similar diversity of schools, a fact many people now recognize. The NCER is deliberating on the question of authorizing community schools, a new type of public school established and operated by the community. This is certainly worthwhile to consider.

To enable creative ideas to be put into practice, I propose that the criteria for approving new types of schools be relaxed. We also need to encourage experimental classes within the existing system and find ways to disseminate information about innovative measures that have been successfully implemented.

Faced with the problems of bullying, violence and absenteeism, the Soka Gakkai's education division has compiled a collection of records of the practical steps its members have taken as teachers to solve problems. This project has been carried out in response to the proposal on education I made sixteen years ago (1984; see "Humanity in Education," p. 161). I was tremendously gratified to hear recently that more than ten thousand such experiences have been compiled, evidence of the painstaking efforts of the teachers over the years. These are precious records and reports on educational methodologies as put into practice in the field and are an extremely beneficial means of sharing teachers' experiences.

Amid growing concern about the "flight from learning," it is now the vital role of education to strive to create the kinds of schools where children can always find the joys of learning and living.

Japan's Ministry of Education initiated this year (2000) a policy whereby a school can apply to become a research development school with the freedom to determine its own curriculum. The system is open to both public and private schools, and the government will provide financial support. I welcome this system in that it encourages creativity and imagination in the classroom. I also believe that analysis of accumulated results and sharing of information will benefit the educational system as a whole.

Interaction between theory and concrete results from experimentation is a prerequisite, and a good example of this is in the work of the American philosopher John Dewey, who enhanced and deepened his educational theories through experience gained at the Chicago Laboratory School.[13] In the same way, Makiguchi's *The System of Value-Creating Pedagogy* and Toda's *Deductive Guide to Arithmetic* are both based on actual practice in the classroom.

Toda, Makiguchi's most loyal supporter and my own mentor, established an elementary tutorial school, the Jishu Gakkan, in 1923 as a place to prove the theory of value-creating education. Makiguchi referred to the Jishu Gakkan as a materialization of his own vision for elementary schools, describing it as the greatest proof of his work. Meanwhile, being determined to continue Toda's work, I have founded a system of schools from the elementary to university and postgraduate levels based on Makiguchi's principles of value-creating education.

Volunteer Activities

In addition to establishing a creative learning environment, it is equally important to cultivate humanism in our children through actual experience in society. One well-documented tendency in modern children is egoistic behavior and attenuated human relationships, while the intensely competitive examination system becomes the sole focus of children's lives. In addition, many are so absorbed in the virtual world of the internet, television and video games that they have become numb to the stimulations offered by the real world.

How can we encourage children to directly communicate with society and nature? One popular idea is involvement in volunteer activities. I believe this should be promoted, not merely through occasional field trips but as continuous ongoing activities. To be specific, there should be activities that produce tangible results — work within the community, such as recycling, that contributes to society and provides a sense of fulfillment, as well as planting trees and flowers and conservation activities that generate concrete results.

Recently, children have been increasingly violent, and the incidence of juvenile crime is rising. Involvement in constructive, creative activities would lead to the well-balanced physical and spiritual growth of children. After engaging in constructive activities and projects, children would return with healthier emotions and peace of mind, bearing out the words of the philosopher William James when he spoke of the need for a "moral equivalent of war"[14] to develop discipline and channel aggression.

In this regard, Makiguchi asserted that, through his vision of a half-day school system, the surplus energy of young people, often directed to antisocial targets, can be used in a way that is of value to society, thus contributing to both individual happiness and the community at the same time. Experiencing the feeling that one's actions are of use to others gives confidence to young people and becomes a firm foundation for spiritual growth.

The year 2001 has been designated as the U.N. International Year of Volunteers. Taking this as an opportunity, we should deepen appreciation of volunteer activities throughout society, not just in the limited environment of the school, and pave a path toward a humanitarian society in the twenty-first century.

Fundamental Reform of Universities

Next, I would like to touch upon the university entrance examination system, a pivotal issue in educational reform in Japan. Currently, as the already excessive pressure of examinations intensifies, one serious problem is the tendency to turn high schools into nothing more than a preparatory stage for entrance to universities. Now that family size is decreasing and the pressure for access to higher education is reduced, Japanese society is presented with a good opportunity to review this system and renew it so it can become truly beneficial to both students and colleges.

What needs to be considered first is diversification of admission processes. I feel there is a need to improve the current university entrance system from a selective screening exam to that of an aptitude test. The method of university admission should not be limited to written entrance examinations. Broader opportunities should be opened through diversified processes such as admission on grounds of special talents and merit; all these efforts should respect and encourage the applicant's will to learn.

The beginning of the university academic year should also be moved from April to September (currently, the academic year in Japan commences in April), both to facilitate smooth transition for exchange students and those returning from studies overseas as well as to provide graduates of Japanese high schools time and various opportunities after graduation and before university entrance. This period could be used as an opportunity to acquire experience in society, read extensively and ponder carefully on life.

Most important is the need to reconsider our approach to education in terms of including both specialization and a well-rounded general education. In a rapidly changing society, academic disciplines are likely to become further subdivided and highly specialized, reducing the weight of basic liberal arts subjects in college curricula. This will limit the breadth of education a student can receive. Liberal arts at Japanese universities are currently lacking a clear-cut goal or principle. I therefore call for a reevaluation of our approach in this crucial area. Simultaneously, we must expand education in specialized fields and ensure coordination with the courses offered at graduate school.

The Contributions of Soka University

It is vital that we define the ideal direction for humanistic education and create a new current of education for the twenty-first century. Soka University of America, Aliso Viejo, will open in 2001 as a liberal arts college focused on providing a well-rounded general education while preparing students to pursue more specialized courses of study, including postgraduate courses. As its founder, I am committed to bold experimentation and full implementation of the ideals of value-creating education.

In all areas of university education, but especially liberal arts, we need to end the tight demarcations among departments and adopt an organic and interdisciplinary approach. For this purpose, faculty members should be urged to drastically reform their teaching methods. One reason many students find classes unattractive is the outdated class content, which is repeated year after year. I have already referred to the dysfunction of the school education system: The problems faced by universities in this regard have also been neglected.

The interim report of the University Council of the Ministry of Education emphasized the need to enhance the teaching abilities of university faculty members. Faculty members must make ceaseless efforts to improve the quality of classes and avoid inertia, to prevent the overall quality of university education from being damaged.

In Japan, Soka University established a Center for Excellence in Teaching and Learning in 2000. The center will support the faculty in various projects to develop innovative teaching methods and also provide students with learning assistance to help them gain the ability to resolve difficulties on their own.

At Soka University of America, meanwhile, every student and faculty member will participate in the Core Curriculum, a

unique series of four courses focusing on central issues facing our world in the twenty-first century:
- What is an individual human life?
- What is the relationship between the individual and the physical environment in which we live?
- What is the relationship between the individual and the human environment in which we live?
- What are the global issues in peace, culture and education?

Each issue will be addressed from a range of perspectives — historical, multicultural, analytical and experiential — so as to provide the foundation for ongoing learning.

In Japan, too, I believe that a liberal arts education should be the core element of the first half of every university degree course, as it provides a general understanding of humanity. For the second half of the course, we need to make university administration more flexible, namely, to introduce a double-major system and establish a system that allows compatibility in credits and transfers between schools to enable students to move to universities in specialized academic fields.

When choosing universities, students in Japan are inclined to prioritize universities or departments that are easy to enter. If this situation persists, it will never generate positive results for either the students or the universities. To avoid this, universities should cooperate in providing classes in areas that students truly wish to pursue. During their time in university, as students' interests develop, they are likely to wish to change to a completely different field, which may require moving to a different university. The current system, however, does not allow the transfer of credits and thus discourages this process.

In response, universities in some parts of Japan are forming alliances enabling the transfer of credits. These are bold and greatly significant reforms for the benefit of students. Ideally, universities should allow individual students to study what they want, when they want and where they want. To achieve this, we need to allow mobility, concentrating on the academic discipline and specialization, not the university. This will form part of the development of a lifelong education system.

Promoting International Exchange

Another task universities should address, I believe, is opening their doors to international exchange. Japan, in particular, urgently needs to promote internationalization in all institutions of higher learning.

Soka University aims to be a new kind of university based on the principles of humanism. For this reason, ever since it was established, it has actively promoted educational exchanges with universities in other countries throughout the world. It has already signed academic exchange agreements with more than seventy universities. Through such exchanges, many students have studied abroad, and regular exchanges of faculty members have been promoted. We are striving toward globalization of the educational environment by enhancing mutual understanding among cultures.

The high standards of American university education compared to those of Japanese universities is often mentioned here. I am convinced that the wellspring of the vigor of American colleges lies in the country's spiritual climate that respects diversity and freedom and welcomes educators and students of many different nationalities.

In Japan, teaching staff have tended to work abroad only for the sake of career advancement, while students often view overseas study purely in terms of future career opportunities. But from the viewpoint of cultural exchange and enhancement of the quality of education in Japan, we urgently need to find ways to increase the flow of incoming exchange students. Scholarships will be an important means of supporting students studying abroad as well as encouraging foreign students to study in Japan. Creating a fuller scholarship system will therefore be crucial from the standpoint of building an identity for Japan as a country that places the utmost priority on education.

On the same theme, I want to emphasize the importance of language education, especially English, at an early stage. Even if we make structural preparations for international exchange at the university level, unless we fundamentally break down the language barrier, the range of exchanges will not expand, and these plans will remain "pie in the sky." Moreover, globalization means that linguistic proficiency is becoming an indispensable ability. Language skills can help to bring the world together. Language is a tool that enables us to expand our chances of learning about the lives and values of people throughout the world as well as promoting heart-to-heart exchanges.

As one concrete measure, it is important to actively promote English education in elementary schools. This, however, should not consist of just bringing forward junior high school English classes but rather focus on learning conversation skills in an enjoyable environment that also deepens understanding of culture. Naturally, we should not neglect the study of Japanese language, history and culture as well.

Toward a Century Radiant With the Smiles of Children

Last, allow me to reemphasize the global challenge that faces us: the creation of a human society that serves the essential needs of education. When defined as those activities that foster the talents and character of human beings, "education" is in no way limited to classrooms but is a mission that must be undertaken and realized by human society as a whole. We must now go back to the original purpose of education — children's lifelong happiness — and reflect upon the state of our respective societies and our ways of living.

What kind of world should we build for our children to inherit? At the threshold of a new century, we have a great opportunity to seriously face these issues — and it is an opportunity we must seize.

The United Nations has designated the first decade of the twenty-first century (2001–10) the International Decade for a Culture of Peace and Nonviolence for the Children of the World. I wholeheartedly welcome this designation since it is a theme I have promoted continuously over the years. UNESCO will be assuming a central role in this campaign, but its success depends on a broad range of popular support and cooperation.

The youth division of the SGI-USA has been engaged in "Victory Over Violence" (VOV), a movement to educate people about nonviolence, since 1999. This movement is conducted through promoting dialogue to disseminate the spirit of nonviolence. The overarching goal is to transform the tendency to downplay the sanctity of life that became deeply rooted in the minds of our children during the twentieth century, the century of war and violence. The VOV movement is developing broadly in American society and receiving support from many human rights organizations, schools and other educational institutions. Above all, it has become a tremendous source of hope and courage for young people who have suffered the effects of violence.

Like the United States, Japan also needs to address this tendency to devalue life. Sensational coverage of tragic incidents, pointing at the darkness in children's hearts, will do nothing to solve the problem. Society's values have become inverted. As adults, we must speak out and take action.

I believe that through such engagement we can construct a value-creating society and live truly nonegoistic lives grounded in mutual respect.

Education separated from society can have no vital force; likewise, there is no future for a society that forgets that education is its true mission. Education is not a mere right or obligation. I believe education in the broadest sense is the mission of every individual. To awaken this awareness throughout society must be the highest priority in all our endeavors.

I conclude by pledging that I will devote all my energy to creating a century in which children's lives will shine with happiness, and the magnificent promise of education will finally be fulfilled.

4

Education Toward Global Citizenship

June 13, 1996, Teachers College, Columbia University

It is with profound emotion that I speak today at the college where the world-renowned philosopher John Dewey taught. The first president of the Soka Gakkai, Tsunesaburo Makiguchi, whose thinking is the founding spirit of Soka University, referenced with great respect the writings and ideas of Dewey in his 1930 work, *The System of Value-Creating Pedagogy*.

My own interest in and commitment to education stem from my experiences during World War II. My four elder brothers were drafted and sent to the front; the eldest was killed in action in Burma. During the two or so years following the end of the war, my three surviving brothers returned one after another from the Chinese mainland. In their tattered uniforms, they were a truly pathetic sight. My parents were already aged; my father's pain and my mother's sadness were searing.

To the end of my days, I will never forget the disgust and anger with which my eldest brother, on leave from China, described the inhuman atrocities he had seen committed there by the Japanese army. I developed a deep hatred for war, its cruelty, stupidity and waste. In 1947, I encountered a superb educator, Josei Toda. Toda, together with his mentor, Makiguchi, was jailed for opposing Japan's wars of invasion. Makiguchi died in jail. Toda survived the two-year ordeal of imprisonment.

When, at nineteen, I learned of this, I instinctively knew that here was someone whose actions merited my trust. I determined to follow Toda as my mentor in life.

It was Toda's constant and impassioned plea that humanity could be liberated from horrific cycles of war only by fostering new generations of people imbued with a profound respect for the sanctity of life. He therefore gave the highest possible priority to the work of education.

Education is a uniquely human privilege. It is the source of inspiration that enables us to become fully and truly human, to fulfill a constructive mission in life with composure and confidence.

The end point in the development of knowledge isolated from human concerns is the weaponry of mass destruction. At the same time, it is knowledge also that has made society comfortable and convenient, bringing industry and wealth. The fundamental task of education must be to ensure that knowledge serves to further the cause of human happiness and peace.

Education must be the propelling force for an eternally unfolding humanitarian quest. For this reason, I consider education the final and most crucially important undertaking of my life. This is also the reason I deeply concur with the view expressed by Teachers College President Arthur Levine that while education is perhaps the slowest means to social change, it is the only means.

Global society today faces myriad, interlocking crises. These include the issues of war, environmental degradation, the North–South development gap and divisions among people based on differences of ethnicity, religion or language. The list is long and familiar, and the road to solutions may seem all too distant and daunting.

It is my view, however, that the root of all of these problems is our collective failure to make the human being — human happiness — the consistent focus and goal in all fields of endeavor. The human being is the point to which we must return and from which we must depart anew. What is required is a human transformation — a human revolution.

There are many areas of commonality in the thinking of Makiguchi and Dewey, and this is one of them. They shared an immovable conviction in the need for new modes of people-centered education. As Dewey put it, "Everything which is distinctly human is learned."[1]

Dewey and Makiguchi were contemporaries. On opposite ends of the Earth, amidst the problems and dislocations of their newly industrializing societies, both wrestled with the task of laying a path toward a hope-filled future.

Greatly influenced by the views of Dewey, Makiguchi asserted that the purpose of education must be the lifelong happiness of learners. He further believed that true happiness is to be found in a life of value creation. Put simply, value creation is the capacity to find meaning, to enhance one's own existence and contribute to the well-being of others, under any circumstance. Makiguchi's philosophy of value creation grew from insights into the inner workings of life that his study of Buddhism afforded him.

Both Dewey and Makiguchi looked beyond the limits of the nation-state to new horizons of human community. Both, it could be said, had a vision of global citizenship, of people capable of value creation on a global scale.

Over the past several decades, I have been privileged to meet and converse with many people from all walks of life, and I have given the matter some thought. Certainly, global citizenship is not determined merely by the number of languages one speaks or the number of countries to which one has traveled.

I have many friends who could be considered quite ordinary citizens but who possess an inner nobility; who have never traveled beyond their native place, yet who are genuinely concerned for the peace and prosperity of the world.

I am confident that the following are essential elements of global citizenship.

- The wisdom to perceive the interconnectedness of all life and living.
- The courage not to fear or deny difference, but to respect and strive to understand people of different cultures and to grow from encounters with them.
- The compassion to maintain an imaginative empathy that

reaches beyond one's immediate surroundings and extends to those suffering in distant places.

The all-encompassing interrelatedness that forms the core of the Buddhist worldview can provide a basis, I feel, for the concrete realization of these qualities of wisdom, courage and compassion.

The following scene from the Buddhist canon provides a beautiful visual metaphor for the interdependence and interpenetration of all phenomena.

Suspended above the palace of Indra, the Buddhist god who symbolizes the natural forces that protect and nurture life, is an enormous net. A brilliant jewel is attached to each of the knots of the net. Each jewel contains and reflects the image of all the other jewels in the net, which sparkles in the magnificence of its totality.

When we learn to recognize what Thoreau refers to as "the infinite extent of our relations,"[2] we can trace the strands of mutually supportive life and discover there the glittering jewels of our global neighbors. Buddhism seeks to cultivate wisdom grounded in this kind of empathetic resonance with all forms of life.

In the Buddhist view, wisdom and compassion are intimately linked and mutually reinforcing.

Compassion in Buddhism does not involve the forcible suppression of our natural emotions, our likes and dislikes. Rather, it is to realize that even those whom we dislike have qualities that can contribute to our lives and can afford us opportunities to grow in our own humanity. Further, it is the compassionate desire to find ways of contributing to the well-being of others that gives rise to limitless wisdom.

Buddhism teaches that both good and evil are potentialities that exist in all people. Compassion consists in the sustained and courageous effort to seek out the good in all people, whoever they may be, however they may behave. It means striving, through sustained engagement, to cultivate the positive qualities in oneself and in others.

Engagement, however, requires courage. There are all too many cases in which compassion, owing to a lack of courage, remains mere sentiment.

Buddhism calls a person who embodies these qualities of wisdom, courage and compassion, who strives without cease for the happiness of others, a bodhisattva. In this sense, it could be said that the bodhisattva provides an ancient precedent and modern exemplar of the global citizen.

The Buddhist canon also includes the story of a contemporary of Shakyamuni, a woman by the name of Srimala, who dedicated herself to education, teaching others that the practice of the bodhisattva consists in encouraging, with maternal care, the ultimate potential for good within all people.

Her vow is recorded thus: "If I see lonely people, people who have been jailed unjustly and have lost their freedom, people who are suffering from illness, disaster or poverty, I will not abandon them. I will bring them spiritual and material comfort."[3]

In concrete terms, her practice consisted of:
- Encouraging others by addressing them with kindness and concern through dialogue.

- Giving alms, or providing people with the things they require.
- Taking action on behalf of others.
- Joining with others and working together with them.

Through these efforts she sought to realize her goal of bringing forth the positive aspects of those she encountered.

The practice of the bodhisattva is supported by a profound faith in the inherent goodness of people. Knowledge must be directed to the task of unleashing this creative, positive potential. This purposefulness can be likened to the skill that enables one to make use of the precision instruments of an airplane to reach a destination safely and without incident.

For this reason, the insight to perceive the evil that causes destruction and divisiveness — and that is equally part of human nature — is also necessary. The bodhisattva's practice is an unshrinking confrontation with what Buddhism calls the fundamental darkness of life. [4]

"Goodness" can be defined as that which moves us in the direction of harmonious coexistence, empathy and solidarity with others. The nature of evil, on the other hand, is to divide: people from people, humanity from the rest of nature.

The pathology of divisiveness drives people to an unreasoning attachment to difference and blinds them to human commonalties. This is not limited to individuals but constitutes the deep psychology of collective egoism, which takes its most destructive form in virulent strains of ethnocentrism and nationalism.

The struggle to rise above such egoism and live in larger and more contributive realms of selfhood constitutes the core of the bodhisattva's practice. Education is, or should be, based on the same altruistic spirit as the bodhisattva.

The proud mission of those who have received an education must be to serve, in seen and unseen ways, the lives of those who have not had this opportunity. At times, education may become a matter of titles and degrees and the status and authority these confer. I am convinced, however, that education should be a vehicle to develop in one's character the noble spirit to embrace and augment the lives of others.

Education should provide in this way the momentum to win over one's own weaknesses, to thrive in the midst of society's sometimes stringent realities, and to generate new victories for the human future.

The work of fostering global citizens, laying the conceptual and ethical foundations of global citizenship, concerns us all. It is a vital project in which we all are participants and for which we all share responsibility. To be meaningful, education for global citizenship should be undertaken as an integral part of daily life in our local communities.

Like Dewey, Makiguchi focused on the local community as the place where global citizens are fostered. In his 1903 work, *The Geography of Human Life*, considered a pioneering work in social ecology, Makiguchi stressed the importance of the community as the site of learning.

Elsewhere Makiguchi wrote: "The community, in short, is the world in miniature. If we encourage children to observe directly the complex relations between people and the land, between nature and society, they will grasp the realities of their homes, their school, the town, village or city, and will be able to understand the wider world."[5]

This is consonant with Dewey's observation that those who have not had the kinds of experience that deepen understanding of neighborhood and neighbors cannot maintain regard for people of distant lands.[6]

Our daily lives are filled with opportunities to develop ourselves and those around us. Each of our interactions with others — dialogue, exchange and participation — is an invaluable chance to create value. We learn from people and it is for this reason that the humanity of the teacher represents the core of the educational experience.

Makiguchi argued that humanistic education, education that guides the process of character formation, is a transcendent skill that might best be termed an art. Makiguchi's initial experience as a teacher was in a remote, rural region of Japan, where he taught in the Japanese equivalent of a one-room schoolhouse. The children were poor, and the manners they brought from their impoverished homes rough.

Makiguchi, however, was insistent: "They are all equally students. From the viewpoint of education, what difference could there be between them and other students? Even though they may be covered with dust or dirt, the brilliant light of life shines from their soiled clothes. Why does no one try to see this? The teacher is all that stands between them and the cruel discrimination of society."[7]

The teacher is the most important element of the educational environment. This creed of Makiguchi's is the unchanging spirit of Soka education.

Elsewhere, he writes: "Teachers should come down from the throne where they are ensconced as the object of veneration to become public servants who offer guidance to those who seek to ascend to the throne of learning. They should not be masters who offer themselves as paragons but partners in the discovery of new models."[8]

It is my abiding conviction that it is the teacher dedicated to serving students, and not the inanimate facility, that makes a school.

I recently heard an educator offer this view: Students' lives are not changed by lectures but by people. For this reason, interactions between students and teachers are of the greatest importance.

In my own case, most of my education was under the tutelage of my mentor in life, Josei Toda. For some ten years, every day before work, he taught me a curriculum of history, literature, philosophy and organization theory. On Sundays, our one-on-one sessions started in the morning and continued all day. He was constantly questioning me — *interrogating* might be a better word — about my reading.

Most of all, however, I learned from his example. The burning commitment to peace that remained unshaken throughout his imprisonment was something he carried with him his entire life. It was from this, and from the profound compassion that characterized each of his interactions, that I most learned.

Ninety-eight percent of what I am today I learned from him.

The Soka, or value-creating, education system was founded out of a desire that future generations should have the opportunity to experience this same kind of humanistic education. It is my greatest hope that the graduates of the Soka schools will become global citizens who can author a new history for humankind.

The actions of such citizens will not be effective unless coordinated, and in this regard we cannot ignore the important potential of the United Nations system.

We have reached the stage where the United Nations can serve as a center, not only for "harmonizing the actions of nations"[9] but also for creating value through the education of global citizens who can create a world of peace. While states and national interests have dominated debate at the world organization to date, increasingly, the energy of "We the people . . ." has been making itself felt, particularly through the activities of nongovernmental organizations.

In recent years, global discourse on such critical issues as the environment, human rights, indigenous peoples, women and population has been held under U.N. auspices. With the participation of both governmental and nongovernmental representatives, conferences on world issues have furthered the process of shaping the kind of global ethic that must undergird global citizenship.

In coordination with ongoing efforts of the United Nations in this direction, I would hope to see these issues incorporated as integral elements of education at all levels. For example:

- Peace education, in which young people learn the cruelty and folly of war, to root the practice of nonviolence in human society.
- Environmental education, to study current ecological realities and means of protecting the environment.
- Developmental education, to focus attention on issues of poverty and global justice.
- Human rights education, to awaken an awareness of human equality and dignity.

I have long believed that education must never be subservient to political interests. To this end, I feel that education should be accorded a status within public affairs equivalent even to that of the legislative, executive or judicial branches of government. This proposal grows out of the experiences of my predecessors, the first and second presidents of the Soka Gakkai, who fought consistently against political control of education.

In the coming years, I hope that we will see the realization of a world summit, not of politicians, but of educators. This is because nothing is of greater importance to humanity's future than the transnational solidarity of educators.

Toward that end, we are determined to continue our efforts to promote educational exchange among young people, following the example of Teachers College, which I understand at present has a student body drawn from some eighty countries.

As Makiguchi stated, "Educational efforts built on a clear understanding and with a defined sense of purpose have the power to overcome the contradictions and doubts that plague humankind and to bring about an eternal victory for humanity."[10]

I pledge my fullest efforts to working, together with my distinguished friends and colleagues gathered here today, toward fostering the kind of global citizens who alone can produce this "eternal victory of humanity."

5

An Outspoken Advocate of Educational Reform

June 4, 1996, Simon Wiesenthal Center

It is an unparalleled honor to have this opportunity to speak about the life of Tsunesaburo Makiguchi, the teacher of my teacher and first president of the Soka Gakkai, here at the Simon Wiesenthal Center — a fortress dedicated to the noble mission of protecting peace and human rights. I would like to share with you the convictions for which Makiguchi gave his life, focusing on the two themes of "righteous anger" and "active tolerance."

The following quotes from Makiguchi's writings will suffice to indicate the degree to which his thinking ran counter to that of Japanese militarism — the prevailing mood of his times.

"Rebuking and removing evil is part and parcel of embracing and protecting good."

"If you cannot be a courageous enemy of evil, you cannot be a friend to the good."

"One must not be satisfied with passive goodness; one must be a person of courage and mettle who can actively strive for good."[1]

Makiguchi opposed Japan's role in World War II and the restrictions the military government imposed on freedom of religion. As a consequence, he was jailed, abused and died in prison at seventy-three.

Tsunesaburo Makiguchi was born in 1871 in a small village on the Sea of Japan in Niigata Prefecture. The name of the village was Arahama, which might be translated as "beach of rough seas."

Makiguchi proudly referred to his humble origins, his birth in an impoverished fishing village. The poverty of his family and the need to support them forced him to give up further study after elementary school. Nevertheless, he utilized every opportunity for reading and learning and showed great talent for teaching. Because of his scholarly disposition, a small sum of money was contributed by those with whom he worked so that he could go to a teachers' college, from which he graduated at twenty-two.

Makiguchi poured his youthful energy and passion into the task of expanding educational opportunity for his underprivileged students. Many of those who were taught by Makiguchi have left grateful descriptions of his efforts as a teacher.

During Makiguchi's days as a young teacher, Japan began pursuing a national policy expressed by the slogan "national wealth and military strength"—the path of imperial expansion. In the field of education, highest priority was likewise accorded to national aims, and all efforts were made to instill a blind, unquestioning patriotism.

Makiguchi, by contrast, expressed this view: "What then is the purpose of national education? Rather than devise complex theoretical interpretations, it is better to start by looking to the lovely child who sits on your knee and ask yourself: What can I do to assure that this child can lead the happiest life possible?"[2]

Makiguchi's focus of interest was never the state but always people, individual human beings. This reflects his strong sense of human rights, which inspired him to declare, in an era when the priorities of state sovereignty were being forcefully emphasized, that "the freedom and rights of the individual are sacred and inviolable."[3]

In 1903, at thirty-two, Makiguchi published his thousand-page work, *The Geography of Human Life*. This publication came on the eve of the Russo–Japanese war. The tenor of the times is symbolized by the fact that seven of Japan's most famous scholars from Tokyo Imperial University petitioned the government to take a hard-line stance against Russia, heightening public enthusiasm for war. In contrast, Makiguchi, an unknown schoolteacher, was promoting an awareness as global citizens who, while rooted in the local community, avoid the pitfalls of narrow-minded nationalism.

At forty-two, Makiguchi was appointed principal of an elementary school in Tokyo. For the next twenty years, he served in this capacity, developing some of Tokyo's most outstanding public schools.

One important influence on Makiguchi's thinking was the American philosopher John Dewey, whose philosophy he sought to use to create change in the Japanese educational system. An outspoken advocate of educational reform, Makiguchi found himself under the constant scrutiny and pressure of the authorities. Among his controversial proposals was a call to abolish the system of official inspection through which representatives of the central bureaucracy could directly interfere in the running of local schools.

He also refused to give in to the prevailing custom of granting special treatment to the children of influential families. This eventually resulted in a leading national politician lobbying for Makiguchi's ouster. Students, teachers and parents all rallied to Makiguchi's defense and sought unsuccessfully to have the transfer order stayed, even staging a boycott of classes. At the school to which Makiguchi was transferred, he met with similar harassment. This time, he made the educational authorities renovate a playground as a condition for accepting the transfer.

Makiguchi's endeavors bring to mind the great love of humanity demonstrated by his contemporary, the extraordinary Jewish–Polish educator Janusz Korczak, who fought to the very end to protect the lives of his students, dying together with them in the Holocaust.

In 1928, Makiguchi encountered Buddhism. Buddhism, in that it recognizes and seeks to develop the wisdom inherent in all human beings, can be considered a philosophy of popular education. Makiguchi felt that in Buddhism he had found the means by which to realize the ideals he had pursued throughout his life — a movement for social reform through education.

Makiguchi was already fifty-seven when he embraced Buddhism — an event that commences the dramatic final developments of his life.

Two years later, on November 18, 1930, together with his disciple and fellow teacher, Josei Toda, Makiguchi published the first volume of *The System of Value-Creating Pedagogy*, and it is from this day that we date the establishment of our organization.

Soka is Japanese for "value creation." From Makiguchi's viewpoint, the most fundamental and central value is that of life itself. Taking into account Dewey's pragmatism, he stated that "The only value in the true sense is that of life itself. All other values arise solely within the context of interaction with life."[4] The fundamental criterion for value, in Makiguchi's view, is whether something adds to or detracts from, advances or hinders, the human condition.

The ultimate goal of Soka, or value-creating, education is to foster people of character who continuously strive for the greatest good — that of peace — who are committed to protecting the sanctity of life and who are capable of creating value under even the most difficult circumstances.

In 1939, what was in effect the first general meeting of the Soka Kyoiku Gakkai (Value-Creating Education Society) was held. This was the year in which World War II began with the Nazi invasion of Poland. Japan's armies were also on the move, committing horrible barbarities in China and Korea.

Deeply disturbed by these developments, Makiguchi launched a frontal critique of militarist fascism. At the time, most religions and religious organizations in Japan lent their support to State Shinto, which provided the philosophical and spiritual underpinnings for the prosecution of the war. Makiguchi, however, opposed this trampling underfoot of the freedoms of conscience and belief, refusing to permit his religious convictions to deviate from their orientation toward peace.

He was also outraged by the attempt to impose belief in Japanese Shinto on the peoples of Asia, writing, "The arrogance of the Japanese people knows no bounds."[5] His stern and uncompromising attitude in this regard stemmed from a profound spirit of tolerance toward the cultural and religious heritage of other peoples.

In December 1941, Japan's forces made a surprise attack on Pearl Harbor, thus initiating the war in the Pacific. Five months later, the periodical of the Soka Kyoiku Gakkai, *Kachi Sozo* (Value Creation), was forced to cease publication at the order of the domestic security authorities.

Having deprived the Japanese people of their freedoms of conscience and religion, it was a simple task for the fascist military powers to suppress freedom of speech. By depriving people of their fundamental freedoms, the military authorities sought to create an obedient, sheep-like mass. Makiguchi expressed his firm conviction that "a single lion will triumph over a thousand sheep. A single person of courage can achieve greater things than a thousand cowards."[6] Makiguchi's stance squarely confronting all forms of evil and injustice made his ideas a potent threat to the powers that be. He was considered a thought criminal, and his activities were subject to constant surveillance by the secret police.

Nevertheless, Makiguchi continued to organize small discussion meetings where he openly expressed his religious and moral convictions. According to his written indictment, he attended over the course of two wartime years more than 240 such meetings. In the presence of the police during these meetings, Makiguchi continued to criticize military fascism. Often police would cut his speeches short.

When even the priests who professed to share Makiguchi's Buddhist faith capitulated to government pressure to pray to the Shinto talisman, Makiguchi refused to the very last.

In July 1943, Makiguchi and Toda were arrested by militarist Japan's equivalent of the Gestapo. They were charged with violations of the notorious "Peace Preservation Act"[7] and with *lèse-majesté*, disrespect for the emperor. Makiguchi was already seventy-two and spent the next year and four months, a total of five hundred days, in solitary confinement.

Makiguchi, however, never retreated a step. It is said that he used to call out from his solitary cell, asking the other prisoners if they were bored, offering to engage them in debate about such questions as whether there is any difference between not doing good and actually committing wrong.[8] He was an unrestrained master of humanistic education who always sought equal and unqualified dialogue with others.

He even explained, patiently and clearly, the principles of Buddhism to his guards and interrogators. The official deposition records his view that a way of life in which one is "so sensitive to the praise or censure of society that, while not doing evil, one fails to do good" runs, in the final analysis, counter to the teachings of Buddhism.[9]

There is a famous Buddhist aphorism that if you light a lamp for another, your own path will be brightened.[10] Indeed, Makiguchi was to the very end an example of a life of positive contribution, bringing forth the brilliant light of hope for himself and for others.

Elsewhere in the record of his interrogations we find him declaring Japan's invasion of China and the "Great East Asian War" a "national catastrophe" brought on by the fundamental spiritual misorientation of the Japanese nation. At a time when Japan's invasions were described as a "sacred war" and the press and opinion-makers were vying to glorify this undertaking, Makiguchi's words reflect a singular courage and determination.

His prison letters to his family have survived, and in them we find such passages as these:

> "For the present, aged as I am, this is where I will cultivate my mind."

> "I am able to read books, which is a pleasure. I want for nothing. Please watch over the home in my absence, and don't concern yourselves about me."

> "Being in solitary confinement, I can ponder things in peace, which I prefer."[11]

His letters are filled with concern and consideration for his family; in them, one senses composure, even optimism. "Even hell has its enjoyments, depending on one's outlook," he wrote in a passage scratched out by the prison censors.

The hell of the four walls of his stifling solitary cell, its heat and cold, took a steady toll on Makiguchi's aged frame. But he was never despondent; in his heart, the brilliant sun of his beliefs rose and remained high. Burning with righteous anger, Makiguchi continued his struggle against the forces of a state authority that refused to respect human rights. His anger, however, was never tainted with hatred.

Inevitably, age and malnutrition brought physical decline, and Makiguchi finally agreed to be transferred to the infirmary. Donning his formal clothes, he straightened his hair and walked there unaided, with frail yet determined step. The following day, on November 18, 1944, the anniversary of the founding of the Soka Gakkai, Tsunesaburo Makiguchi died peacefully.

Not even the terror of death could force Makiguchi into submission.

For human beings, nothing is perhaps more universally dreaded than the prospect of one's own demise. It could even be said that fear of death forms the basis for instinctual aggression. Yet Buddhism speaks of the indivisible unity of life and death, asserting that these are both integral aspects of an eternal continuum. For one who lives with just and unwavering conviction, and has a penetrating understanding of the essential nature of life and death, both life and death can be experienced as joys.

In the frigid confines of prison, Makiguchi proved the truth that by living with utter dedication to humane and noble ideals, it is possible to greet death without a trace of fear, regret or loathing. Unknown to anyone, he brought to completion the life he had made great by his actions and his spirit.

His quiet passing was at the same time a new start, a new departure.

Josei Toda spoke of the unbearable grief and outrage that seized him when, two months later, one of the judges bluntly informed him, "Makiguchi's dead." He spoke of moaning in solitude, of crying until his tears ran dry.

But, from the depths of this despair, new hope was born.

Toda the disciple emerged alive from the prison where his mentor had died. Anger at the authoritarian forces that had robbed his mentor of life was transformed into a pledge and determination to create a new popular movement for peace.

In *The System of Value-Creating Pedagogy*, Makiguchi wrote: "Driven by their instinct for self-preservation, evil-minded people band together, increasing the force with which they persecute the good. In contrast, people of goodwill always seem to be isolated and weak.... There is no alternative but for people of goodwill to unite."[12] This was his penetrating insight based on personal experience.

As a disciple sharing profound unity of purpose with his mentor, Josei Toda began, amidst the postwar devastation, to construct a movement based on the solidarity of ordinary citizens of goodwill. Again, his methodology was grass-roots — one-on-one dialogue and small-scale discussion meetings.

Grounded on the principle of the sanctity of life as expounded in Buddhism, this is a movement that seeks to empower people, to awaken their inner wisdom, thus creating a world in which justice and humane values are accorded universal respect.

In his theory of value, Makiguchi states that the existence of religion is justified by the degree to which it relieves suffering and brings happiness to individuals (the value of gain) and to societies (the value of goodness). In his unalloyed humanism, he asserted that people do not exist to serve religion; religion exists to serve people.

6

Teachers of My Childhood

From the book *One by One* by Daisaku Ikeda in 2004

When spring arrives, heaven and earth, towns and cities—everything takes on a new brightness. The fresh faces of the students just starting school as the cherry blossoms burst into bloom are also bright and shining.

Although many people delight in the beautiful blossoms, few bother to consider the roots that make this blossoming possible. In life, our roots are largely formed by our first experience in education, the years we spend in elementary school.

"Blooming, blooming, the cherry trees are blooming…." I remember my very first school textbook when I entered elementary school in the spring of 1934. Opening it with excitement, I saw a beautiful spring scene of cherry trees in bloom. In the distance there were mountains, and in the foreground the lovely pink cherry blossoms. This elementary school reader was the first textbook in Japan to be printed in color; it had just come into use the year before I started school.

"Blooming, blooming"—our teacher wrote the words in big letters on the blackboard. Miss Tejima was tall and slim. Many people, I would imagine, retain a clear memory of their elementary school teachers. I, too, recall Miss Tejima with great clarity—the color of her clothing, her hairstyle and even her characteristic gestures. On one occasion, Miss Tejima selected me and just one other student from our entire school year and praised our compositions, saying that they were very well written. I was a little embarrassed to be singled out, but I was also very pleased. Everyone is happy when praised sincerely. It builds confidence. Indeed, Miss Tejima's praise may well have influenced my desire to become a writer.

Changing Times

I attended Haneda Elementary School No. 2 in Tokyo, which at the time was a two-story, wooden building surrounded by rice paddies. On frosty winter days, the water in the paddies sometimes froze. On such days, a rowdy band of children, we would stray off the road and, shouting "This way! This way!" cut through the paddies on our way to school. It was a tranquil, idyllic time.

But things were changing quickly. Japan was entering a dark, oppressive period in its history. The Manchurian Incident[1], which began Japan's invasion of China, took place when I was three. When I was four, there was an abortive coup d'état in which the prime minister was assassinated, and when I was five, Japan withdrew from the League of Nations. Young as we were, we didn't understand what was going on in the world, but the rising waves of the troubled times reached even into our classrooms. A few pages after the blooming cherries in our reader was a page with the barking command: "Advance! Advance! Soldier, advance!"

Another spring came around, and once more the season of cherry blossoms arrived. About this time, my father suffered an attack of debilitating rheumatism and became bedridden. We were forced to scale back our family business processing seaweed; our lives grew harder day by day. My eldest brother had enjoyed good grades, but he was forced to quit school and go to work to contribute to the family finances.

In the third and fourth grades, I had my first male teacher, Mr. Takeuchi. He had just graduated from teachers college and was young and energetic. He placed a particularly heavy emphasis on physical education: "You can be as smart as you like, but if you don't build a strong body when you're young, you'll be of no use to anyone as an adult. Health is important. Study is important. True education combines both." This appears to have been his credo as a teacher.

I was on the short side and not very strong, so it was no easy thing to meet Mr. Takeuchi's expectations. To this day, I am moved whenever I remember how keenly he encouraged me to develop my physical strength and become healthy. I also remember how he taught us about the meaning of the Olympics, explaining in detail how they were conducted. That was in 1936, the year the Berlin Olympics were held in Germany. Mr. Takeuchi stressed the importance of holding the Olympics on a grand scale every four years as a means of promoting world peace.

He clearly hated war. I believe that, in the depths of his heart, he strongly opposed the militaristic trend of the times, believing in the importance of peace and encouraging children to grow into fine individuals with a true love of peace.

Watching Over Growth

In Japan, people who tend and care for cherry trees are called *sakuramori*, a word that implies a sense of careful stewardship. The *sakuramori* look after the cherry trees, encouraging them to grow, tending to their welfare and generally caring for them throughout the four seasons. The care they extend expresses faith in the power of life as it grows and develops into the future. They don't fuss too much about the trees, but at the same time they never ignore them. They observe the trees' growth in great detail but allow them to develop freely. For example, if we stake a tree from the very beginning, the tree will rely on the stakes for support and not grow strong on its own.

The roots are especially important. One expert on trees says that the spread of the crown of a cherry tree is mirrored almost exactly by the spread of its roots below ground. If we water the tree only around the base of the trunk, the tree will become "lazy" and not bother to spread its roots far in search of water.

For people, "roots" correspond to the tenacity of our spirit, our refusal to give up. Once a tree has taken firm root, it can survive even on a rocky mountain face buffeted by powerful winds.

Trees are living things. They are not machines. Every cherry tree is unique. They each grow and thrive in different environments. That is why there is no manual that can tell us how to grow a cherry tree. The only way to succeed is to learn the particular tree's character and idiosyncrasies and, taking them into account, warmly care for it.

Each child is also unique. Each has a distinct way of flowering that is his or hers alone. To raise trees or to foster people, we need patient faith in their potential to flourish. A child who has poor grades or who is out of control and behaving badly now may in the future grow into a person who does truly remarkable things. It is not at all rare for a child we think we know very well to suddenly change and show us a side we never would have imagined. To the precise degree that we care for and have faith in children, they will extend and spread their roots. And it is this that will give them the strength to survive and make their way successfully through life.

Protection, as in "protection of the natural environment," assumes that nature is frail and therefore needs our protection. But stewardship expresses a spirit of awe and respect for the potential for limitless growth. I believe that such awe and respect for children should be the foundation of education.

Vivid Memories

My teacher in the fifth and sixth grades was Mr. Hiyama. I think he was about twenty-five or twenty-six at the time. His broad forehead and clear, bright eyes gave an impression of intellect and acuity. His classes were sometimes challenging, but they were always interesting. Between classes, he would read Eiji Yoshikawa's samurai tale *Musashi* to us, gesturing and posing and reading with dramatic expression, bringing the story alive. We were pulled entirely into the world portrayed in the novel; we could see Musashi dashing about and rival swordsman Kojiro brandishing his sword right before our eyes. It took a year, but Mr. Hiyama read the novel to us in its entirety.

During one class, he spread out a large world map before us and asked us where we wanted to go. I pointed to the middle of the vast expanse of Asia. "I see!" he said. "You have pointed to Dunhuang. There are many wonderful treasures there." From that moment a fascination with Dunhuang—the oasis city on the silk trade routes famous for its temples and painted grottos—took hold in my mind.

I may have pointed to China because my eldest brother, whom I loved and respected, had been sent there as a soldier. He was drafted when I was a fourth grader. After him, my next two older brothers were called up for military service.

My father's rheumatism was improving, but with my three brothers away we were short of help and our family finances got worse and worse. When I was a fifth grader, we had to sell our house and move to a smaller one in the same area. The original house had a large yard with a big pond and a tall cherry tree. Whenever I looked up from beneath the cherry tree in our yard, it seemed as if countless bell-shaped flowers were falling from the bright blue spring sky. It was hard to say goodbye to that big tree, but I was glad that I didn't have to change schools because of the move.

A Teacher's Kindness

Hoping to do what I could to help my family, I got a job delivering newspapers. I woke up each morning while it was still dark and helped out with the seaweed production. When I finished, I delivered my papers and then went to school. After returning from school, I helped with the family business again, pulling the dried sheets of *nori* seaweed off the racks. Then I delivered the evening paper. At night there was the work of cleaning the seaweed, removing any impurities. I look back now on those busy days with fondness.

When I was in sixth grade, we took a school trip to Kansai. We were away for four nights and five days. It was my first trip away from home, and I was very excited. My mother had given me some pocket money, which she had somehow managed to scrape together. I used it to treat my friends, and at the end of the first day it was almost gone. Mr. Hiyama must have been watching me the whole time, because he called to me as I was going up the stairs of the inn where we were staying and said: "Daisaku, your elder brothers are all away at the war. You have to buy your parents a souvenir from your trip."

I was crushed; of course he was right. My mother's face appeared before my eyes. Smiling, Mr. Hiyama placed some money in my palm and closed my fingers around it. I think it was two one-yen bills. At that time, it was a large amount of money. I was happy. I breathed a sigh of relief. When I returned home and gave my mother her gift, I told her what had happened. "You must never forget Mr. Hiyama," she said with a gentle smile.

I don't feel that he was giving me special treatment. He wouldn't have been as well loved as he was by so many students if he was the kind of teacher who had favorites. He cared for us all equally, looking deep into our hearts, aware of the family situations that were the soil that nourished us. I will never forget the warm affection with which he looked at each of us during our graduation ceremony, large tears running down his cheeks.

In 1940, I graduated from elementary school and entered Haneda Higher Elementary School. My teacher for the next two years was Mr. Okabe, whom we called "Mr. Buccaneer."

He was from Okayama in the western part of Japan and used to make us laugh by telling us that in a past life he must have been the leader of a pirate crew sailing the Inland Sea, which was near his hometown. He was tall with jet-black hair and a handsome, intelligent face. There were some forty boys in our class—no girls. Mr. Okabe often encouraged me to exercise to strengthen myself physically. He loved sumo wrestling and taught us various sumo techniques. Even though I was small, I did my best. In the summer, we would take off our shirts and run to the Tama River to swim.

At first glance, Mr. Okabe appeared very intimidating, but I never felt afraid of him. It may have been because I was rather shy, but I can't remember him ever scolding me. Once one of the students in our class was hit by another teacher. When Mr. Okabe heard about it, he charged into the staff room shouting, "Which one of you hit one of my students?" He had a very strong sense of right and wrong. He may have seemed gruff on the outside, but we all felt his concern and affection.

Growing Nationalism

When I was in my second year at Haneda Higher Elementary School, its name was changed to Haginaka National People's School. This was mandated by the National People's School Order, a law filled with militaristic overtones that sought to turn children into soldiers. Terms such as "loyal subjects of the Emperor," "drilling" and "group training" became staples of school life, and the gymnasiums of many schools were converted into martial arts training halls. Japan was sliding down the slope from war with China into the even more disastrous Pacific War. In their arrogance and stupidity, the leaders of the day had no thought for the welfare of ordinary citizens. They were driving the nation into the abyss of war with a mix of threats and well-crafted slogans.

Life became harder with each passing day, and cherry trees, whose wood burned well, were cut down one after another for fuel. The tree in our old garden that I loved so dearly was cut down, and a factory for military supplies was built where it had stood.

Education has a truly astonishing power to cast a spell over the innocent hearts of children. Many of the students in my class at the new "national people's school" applied to enlist as soldiers or as civilian colonists on the Chinese mainland. They did this because it seemed to be the highest expression of patriotism: to be a pioneering hero of the new era. I, too, wanted to become a student pilot in the navy after I graduated. Although I was concerned about my family and how they would fare without me, I secretly sent in an application.

"That's Enough!"

I wasn't there when a representative of the navy visited my home. My father sent the man away, saying: "My three eldest sons are all in the army. The fourth will be going soon. Do you really plan to take away my fifth as well? No more. That's enough!"

When I got home, my father berated me fiercely. I was never so harshly scolded before or after. It gave me a glimpse of my father's true feelings, which he usually kept to himself.

After graduating, I went to work at the Niigata Steelworks. The war situation had worsened and there was an intensifying sense of impending defeat. In 1945, the last year of the war, air raids on Tokyo started on New Year's Day. Our days were filled with war and air raids. Even so, when spring arrived, the cherry trees that remained began blossoming, honest and true to their nature as always.

On the night of April 15, when the cherry petals were starting to fall, southern Tokyo was attacked in a massive air raid. The anguished sound of the air-raid sirens wailed, and mighty B-29s appeared like majestic conquerors, flying steady and low across the sky. The staccato of the strafing from the American planes combined with people's screams. Incendiary bombs fell like a heavy rain. Tongues of flame leapt up here and there, burning madly. In an instant, the entire area was a sea of raging fire, and everyone was desperately trying to flee the conflagration. Parents were separated from small children. Sons and daughters struggled in vain to save elderly parents. All those caught up in this hellish nightmare of death and destruction were filled with searing anguish. Even now, it brings unendurable pain to write of that night.

When the sun rose the next morning, the entire area where I lived had been burned to the ground. Except for Haneda Airport, the town had been reduced to ashes. Both my beloved elementary school and the so-called national people's school had been razed.

Around this time, I found myself walking alone, lost in thought. The war dragged on. What would happen to Japan? What would become of my family? How would I live my life? I could not envision a future. Eventually, I found myself in a small section of town that hadn't burned. A little group of cherry trees was in fragrant bloom. It was like a quiet and peaceful dream. In the vast expanse of burnt-out gray, the beautiful colors of the cherry trees glowed like a torch. In the midst of so much death, here was the light of shining life. "Blooming, blooming, the cherry trees are blooming…."

Words on a Wall

In those days, even cherry trees were made into symbols of death. The Japanese people were told to be like cherry blossoms, to scatter courageously in the wind without a whisper of regret. But the cherry trees before me clearly rejected such perversion and spoke to me—powerfully, sublimely—of life. They were overflowing with hope.

"Live! Live fully and deeply! Never cease living! Outlive the winter and let your own unique nature bloom," they said to me. Powerful emotions welled up and filled my heart. On the wall of a burnt-out factory building, I used a piece of chalk to write a passage from a poem that I composed. Many people carried chalk with them in those days so that in an emergency they could leave a message that would enable their families to find them. I didn't bother signing my poem; later I saw that others who shared my feelings had written their thoughts below mine on the wall.

A poet once wrote: "Blossoms that scatter, blossoms that remain. Even these will scatter." I had not scattered but had survived and was now seventeen. The war had for too long kept me from school and learning. I was filled with the desire to study, to learn, to read books.

I have never forgotten the beloved teachers of my youth. I have stayed in touch with a number of them to this day. Mr. Okabe once wrote to me, exhorting me to live strongly and tenaciously in the face of all obstacles. In another letter he encouraged me, saying: "The taller a tree grows, the harder the wind blows against it. Please endure the wind and snow."

I was able to have a reunion with Mr. Hiyama in Tochigi in 1973. He and his wife traveled an hour and a half by bus to see me. I hadn't seen him for more than thirty years, but he still had the aura of a great educator who had made a fine job of raising many children.

"You don't seem to have any time to rest," he said. "Please be careful not to harm your health." His gaze was just as warm and caring as it had been on that school trip long ago.

Sitting in front of him, I felt as if I had returned to my elementary school days. To a student, your teacher is always your teacher, and to a teacher, your students are always your students. How wonderful it is to have a true teacher! It is easy to encounter a teacher who imparts knowledge, but hard to encounter one who teaches you how to live.

Elementary education is the most critical. But how should we teach elementary school students? It is a very difficult job. That is precisely why I have such tremendous respect for elementary school teachers who do succeed in this challenging work. Are high school teachers more important than elementary school teachers? Are university professors more important than high school teachers? Absolutely not. It is just this kind of erroneous thinking that afflicts our society today: Theorists often have the mistaken idea that they are better than practitioners.

Fostering the Future

An architect who theorizes about architecture is in no way superior to a carpenter who can actually build a house. An agricultural expert is not more productive than a farmer who actually grows vegetables or rice. I sometimes think there are too many people who theorize about things and far too few who actually make painstaking efforts to achieve something.

There are many people who love cherries and other flowering trees but few who truly appreciate the efforts of those who work behind the scenes to keep the trees alive and healthy. The life of an educator is also far from glamorous. Teaching is inconspicuous work that doesn't get much attention; it's a matter of continuous hard work and effort. But it is precisely because of such teachers dedicated to fostering the future that the next generation of children can grow up straight and strong. We must never forget this crucially important fact.

In those dark days, when the power of ultranationalist authorities pressed down so heavily on Japanese society, my teachers held up for their students the great light of humanity. Just like teachers today who are earnestly committed to their profession, they firmly embraced their students and shared their lives with them while struggling against the intrusions of political power into the realm of education.

If being blessed with good teachers is one of life's joys, there can be no one happier than I.

7

The Teacher's Art

From the Philippine magazine *Mirror* in 1998

I remember being set a project one summer vacation during elementary school. We had to make something at home and bring it with us for the new term. Being clumsy, I couldn't get anything together and had to return to school embarrassed and empty-handed.

When asked what happened to my project, I stammered out that I had forgotten it at home. To my horror, the teacher told me to go home and bring it back right away. I returned home feeling desperate and miserable. Looking around, I saw a bookshelf my older brother had made. I presented this to the teacher, who praised my work and gave me a good grade for it. But, looking back, I am sure that he knew the real story.

From one perspective, you might say that this teacher was rewarding me for lying, but that is not my view. Through the warm, big-hearted way he embraced me, he communicated to me a very concrete sense that he believed in me—really what I needed at that moment. And, of course, I felt deeply ashamed and vowed never to let such a thing happen again.

I believe that education is what remains long after the content of each specific lesson we were taught has been forgotten. The essence of education is character formation, teaching young people how to live in society and encouraging them to think independently. Study is much more than simply absorbing existing knowledge and techniques, and the ability to memorize and reason is nothing compared to the wisdom, emotional richness and creativity that reside within every human being.

Education that does not teach a sense of values turns people into mere robots filled with data but with no understanding of what it is for. Such soulless, over-competitive schooling makes successful children arrogant, while the less academically bright are left with little self-confidence and a deep fear of failure.

It is sad that education is often used to cultivate people who are useful only to the extent that they fit into various slots in society, and school systems in Japan and many other countries actually prevent children from developing their full potential.

In the race to climb the ladder of scholastic prestige and status, we can easily lose sight of the most important question of all: What is the purpose of learning?

I believe that the genuine goal of education must be the lifelong happiness of those who learn. Education should never be subordinated to the demands of national ego or of corporations searching for profit-generating employees. Human beings, human happiness, must always be the goal and objective.

My own teacher, Josei Toda, often said that the greatest error of modern humanity was that it confused knowledge with wisdom. Knowledge itself is a neutral tool that can be used for good or evil. As history sadly proves, educated monsters can wreak far greater horror than their unschooled brothers. At least seven of the participants at the Wannsee Conference where the Nazis planned the "final solution"—extermination—to the "Jewish problem" had doctoral degrees. It is hard to imagine a greater perversion and debasement of education.

Wisdom, in contrast, always directs us toward happiness. The task of education must be to stimulate and unleash the wisdom that lies dormant in the lives of all young people. This is not a forced process, like pressing something into a preformed mold, but rather drawing out the potential that exists within.

I firmly believe that every young person has the power within him or her to change the world. It is the role of those who teach to believe in that power, to encourage and release it.

The relationship between teacher and pupil can be a vital link through which new horizons are opened and life develops. To me, the essence of education is this process whereby one person's character inspires another. When teachers become partners in the process of discovery, burning with a passion for truth, the desire to learn will naturally be ignited in their students' hearts. And once children feel that their teachers are genuinely concerned for their individual welfare, they will begin to trust them and open up to them.

It saddens me that now this vital bond between pupil and teacher seems to have been weakened by distrust and misunderstanding. Teachers everywhere struggle with problems of control and discipline, and students resent the fact that they must cram their heads full of knowledge that fails to answer their pressing questions about life, the real world and human relationships.

Teachers who do not understand and care for their students, merely parroting stereotyped answers, cannot possibly satisfy children's curious and sensitive minds. It must never be forgotten that the most important people in a school are its students.

I once heard about a Japanese elementary school teacher who was irritated by a girl in his class who was unable to keep up. He gave up trying to help her after a fellow teacher told him, "Human beings are just like fruit; twenty to thirty percent are always worthless and there's nothing you can do about it."

Then, one day during a break, he noticed the girl playing with a puzzle, trying to put plastic pieces together so they fit into a box. Finally she succeeded and yelled, "I got it," her face sparkling with a delight he had never seen before. The teacher suddenly felt remorse. How dare he give up on her! Wasn't it his job to make sure that each child walked out of his classroom with the confidence that they could do anything if they really tried?

He discovered that the girl's parents, both graduates of leading universities, were constantly calling her "stupid." The teacher resolved to praise her every day, for every little accomplishment, to wash away the stain of criticism from her heart.

After a year, the girl was transformed. Proceeding at her own pace, she came to experience the joy of learning. The key was her realization that if she made an effort to achieve something, she could do it.

This story shows how the smallest failure can destroy a child's confidence, and the smallest catalyst can trigger growth. It is vital that teachers believe in every child's potential and care about their happiness as human beings.

8

An Unforgettable Teacher

From the Philippine magazine *Mirror* in 1998

Tsunesaburo Makiguchi, pioneering Japanese educator and founder of the Soka Gakkai (Value Creation Society), overcame many difficulties in order to study.

He was born in 1870 in a small coastal village and often had to help out in the family business. On busy days, he couldn't go to school, sometimes having to skip classes for several days in a row. But he would always ask a friend about the day's lesson. If his friend had to help out with his own family's work, Makiguchi would say, "I'll do your chores, if you'll tell me what you learned at school today." He would do his friend's share of work and wait on the seashore for him to come back from school.

They would sit on the beach and, using the sand as a blackboard, go over the day's lessons until the sun set. This experience left him acutely conscious of the problems faced by his poorer students, when he became an elementary school teacher himself.

At one point, he was school principal in a very poor area. Concerned about those children whose families couldn't provide them with lunches, he brought lunches for them. But he was concerned for more than just their physical well-being. To preserve their sense of dignity, he left the lunches in a room where students in need could pick them up without drawing attention to themselves.

Makiguchi's initial experience as a teacher was in a remote rural region where he taught in a one-room schoolhouse. The children were poor, and the manners they brought from their impoverished homes were rough. But Makiguchi was insistent, "From the viewpoint of education, what difference could there be between them and other students? Even though they may be covered with dust or dirt, the brilliant light of life shines from their soiled clothes. Why does no one try to see this? The teacher is all that stands between them and the cruel discrimination of society."

He wanted desperately to free children from the Japanese system of teaching by rote learning, which stifled children's individuality. He believed that education should never be forced and saw it as the means to enlighten as many people as possible, providing them with the key to unlock the treasure house of wisdom within themselves.

From his own practical classroom experience, Makiguchi went on to develop his theory of Value-creating Education. For him, the purpose of education was happiness, and the essence of happiness was what he called "value-creation"—*soka* in Japanese. He defined value on three levels: beauty, gain or benefit, and social good. As an educator, he saw his job as enabling young people to create this kind of value for themselves.

Sometimes Makiguchi's theory on education was criticized for being "too down-to-earth."

He retorted: "That's only natural, because the teaching methods I embrace come from my own difficult struggles in the classroom. Mine is not the tenuous theory of a scholar stuck in an office."

Unfortunately, his humane approach contradicted the outlook of Japan's educational system. For instance, in those days it was common for principals and teachers to give special attention to the children of prominent families, to visit them and "pay their respects." Makiguchi refused to follow this corrupt practice and strongly discouraged other teachers from following it. As a result, even though he was extremely popular with the students, he was transferred from one school to the next. Finally, he was forced from the ranks of active teachers.

At the time, Japan's educational system was focused solely on creating obedient servants of the state rather than individuals capable of independent judgment and thinking. While the entire Japanese nation was advancing down the path of nationalism, Makiguchi urged students to dedicate their lives to bringing lasting peace to the entire world.

In 1938, Makiguchi gave a series of lectures on ethics, starting in April, the month when the National Mobilization Law was passed, enlisting all citizens to work toward Japan's war effort. Makiguchi set just one question for the final exam: "What is the purpose of life?"

Out of a possible grade of Excellent, Good or Fair, all the students scored Good. No one received the mark Excellent. When asked why, Makiguchi apparently remarked, looking very disappointed, "Because there was not one person who mentioned world peace in the answer."

It was perhaps unavoidable that Makiguchi should experience conflict with the authorities. Even as Japan became an increasingly militaristic and fascist country, invading and inflicting untold suffering on its Asian neighbors, he continued to speak out. My wife, whose family were early members of the Soka Gakkai educators' society founded by Makiguchi, remembers clearly how he attended a meeting held at their house. Even in the presence of the dreaded secret police, who would cut him short when he became too provocative, he continued to speak out for peace and justice. His courage left a strong impression on my wife.

In July 1943, Makiguchi, together with Josei Toda—his closest supporter and my own teacher—and other leaders of the Soka Gakkai were arrested. Makiguchi was charged with violating the Peace Preservation Law and for failing to show adequate respect to the Emperor. Even under relentless interrogation, he refused to compromise his beliefs. He expressed his Buddhist faith in human equality and his criticism of Japan's war effort, which he called "a national disaster." On November 18, 1944, at age seventy-three, he died in the Tokyo Detention Center.

But Makiguchi's dreams live on today. He had entrusted to Toda the goal of creating a school system in which his educational philosophy could be put into practice. Now the Soka school system—from kindergarten to university level—has been established in Japan, with schools in Hong Kong, Singapore and Malaysia and a university in the United States. Makiguchi's work *The System of Value-Creating Pedagogy* has been translated into four languages. In Brazil and the United States, several mainstream schools have incorporated Mr. Makiguchi's ideas into their teaching methods. They have all had remarkable results.

Makiguchi's focus was always people, individual human beings. He repeatedly called for the people to become wise, to awaken, to find courage and to join forces. As each of us develops and elevates our life from a state of dependence to self-reliance and then to contribution to others, he maintained, we can manifest our full splendor as human beings.

9

Humanity in Education

August 24, 1984

Not a day goes by without serious discussion concerning the lamentable state of our educational system. The problem has reached nationwide proportions. Such phenomena as juvenile delinquency, violence at school, truancy and prevailing lethargy among the young constitute no more than the tip of the iceberg. In spite of the fervent attempts being made both at home and in the schools to deal with it, because of the breadth of the issue, so far no general remedy has been prescribed.

As one person earnestly desiring the wholesome growth and development of youth, I cannot help being anxious. Since I am not a specialist in the field, I have no intention of discussing individual educational methods or the various aspects of the educational system that require reform. All of these things must be handled with wisdom and in the light of world trends and the situation in Japan. Avoiding hastiness, qualified people must approach these problems remaining fully aware that cultivating today's youth will determine the fate of tomorrow's Japan.

Restoring Humanity to Education

Politics, however, must not be allowed to take the lead in educational reforms. In all ages, political power has tended to subjugate education and everything else to its own purposes, as was vividly illustrated by modern Japanese education after the establishment, in 1872, of a system dominated by political aims and giving first priority to the achievement of nationalist goals. Slogans such as "increase production and promote industry" and "enrich the country and strengthen the military" were hoisted aloft like imperial banners to which education was obliged to give service. Though this policy may have been partly justified on the basis of the desire to catch up with the Western powers, we must not avert our eyes from the loss it entailed.

Nor can it be said that the Constitution and the Fundamental Law of Education adopted after World War II succeeded in avoiding the same pitfalls since, generally speaking, politics again took the lead in the postwar democratic education system. Education was once again called on to serve nationalistic aims with the difference that postwar efforts to become a great economic power replaced prewar and wartime efforts to become a great military power. Under such circumstances, when the national aim collapses, educational aims are left dangling in the air. It is therefore by no means coincidental that the dark cloud of educational devastation that engulfed our country from the 1970s into the 1980s coincided with Japan's record of high-rate economic growth and its attendant frustrations.

The true goal of education should be the cultivation of individual character on the basis of respect for humanity. We must admit, however, that in modern Japan education has been used as a means for cultivating people to be of value to the nation and big business; that is, people who will function effectively within the national and economic structure.

For some time I have advocated the establishment of a fourth branch of government — that of education — independent of the present three branches — legislative, executive and judiciary — as a method of dealing with the ills and distortions created by education being dominated by politics. What has been lost in the modern Japanese system of education, led as it has been since the late nineteenth century by political considerations, is humanity.

On the basis of his many years of practice and study in teaching, Tsunesaburo Makiguchi[1] defined education concisely and clearly in the following way. The goal of education must not be set by scholars and must not be taken advantage of by other parties. The goal of education must be one with the goal of life. And this means that it must enable students to attain a life of happiness.

Putting to good use his more than thirty years of experience in practical education and adding to that his astute observations of society, Makiguchi developed a definition of happiness in the form of his original theory of value. He could achieve this because, throughout his life, he kept an enlightened eye turned always on humanity.

In this connection, I am always deeply moved by a passage from the writings of Victor Hugo, the great romanticist who devoted himself to establishing the autonomy of education, to relieving poverty and to ensuring freedom for all: "Light that makes whole. Light that enlightens. All fruitful social impulses spring from knowledge, letters, the arts, and teaching. We must make whole men, *whole* men."

But I do not think we need Hugo's words to realize that the main significance of education is to make "whole men." I insist that all future educational reforms must be made for the sake of humanity, not politics. I further insist that nostalgia — which is sometimes expressed today — for the nationalistic Japanese education of the past is stimulated by doubt concerning the situation of the present and represents that refusal to learn from history.

The question has been argued, and studies and proposals have been made on it from many different angles. But, in my opinion, educational reforms dominated by considerations of humanity must not be made within the framework of the established system but must be guided by these three principles: totality, creativity and internationalization.

Totality of Wisdom

When I speak of totality I mean interrelation. No thing or event exists in isolation; everything is interrelated in some way with everything else to produce one great total image. To take an immediately apparent example, I might cite the human body itself in which the head, hands, torso, legs, internal organs and all individual cells are intimately intermeshed to form the whole. And we cannot overlook the connection between the physical and spiritual. Modern depth psychology and ecology show that interrelations expand infinitely to connect human beings with one another, with the world of nature, and with the entire universe. Inseparably bound, the microcosm and the macrocosm work together in wondrous rhythm.

In the words of Goethe's *Faust*:

> *Lo, single things inwoven, made to blend.*
> *To work in oneness with the whole, and live . . . .*

From ancient times, the ability to perceive the invisible threads interweaving all things has been considered a kind of wisdom. But modern civilization has turned its back on this wisdom and has pursued instead a continual course of fragmentation. Though perhaps an inevitable part of the development of human knowledge, this tendency, while producing noteworthy results in the physical realm, has created a condition in which the cords that once connected individual to individual, to say nothing of the individual and nature, have been severed. And individuals groan in the small, enclosed and lonely spaces to which they have been driven.

In terms of learning and education, this state of affairs can be compared to the way in which humankind has ignored the totality of wisdom and instead has allowed the departmentalization of learning to exist for its own sake. Unrelated to the values of human happiness and a better way of life, learning goes its own way, reaching ever-higher proportions.

The great educator Yukichi Fukuzawa, who lived in the latter half of the nineteenth century when modernization was the major trend in Japan, saw this from a very early date. He once remarked: "This informed person is informed about things but not about the connections among them and is ignorant of the principle mutually connecting this and that. Learning consists solely in understanding mutual relations among things. Learning that does not take such relations into consideration serves no useful purpose."

Further, he observed: "The informed person who does not know connections among things differs from a dictionary only in that he eats and the dictionary does not."

In other words, the person who, like a dictionary, is a compendium of unrelated information knows much but ignores interrelations and is therefore useless and nonconstructive.

Of course, Fukuzawa, the author of *An Encouragement of Learning*, and who studied much himself and stimulated others to do the same, is not attacking learning, but only learning and knowledge for their own sakes. Nor do I think his words reflect pragmatism and practicality alone.

Fukuzawa speaks of connections among things (the Japanese word *en*, which he uses in this meaning, is found in such famous Buddhist terms as *engi*, the pivotal doctrine of causal origination). Determining what connection study and learning have with oneself — that is, what meaning they have — represents an inclination toward the kind of totality of which I have been speaking. This same inclination can be seen in the philosophy of Henri Bergson, who made the famous statement, "Living comes first of all."

Undeniably, the pursuit of learning for learning's sake has

been a great driving force in the development of modern science. But, in the light of such results as the development of nuclear weapons and environmental pollution, we are compelled to examine the social responsibility of scientists. Scientists must ask themselves what connection their learning has with their own fate and with that of all humankind.

On the more practical plane of actual education, I often hear of students who no longer read great classics and literary masterpieces but content themselves with digests giving all the information they need to pass literature-course examinations. They know no more than the digests tell them and have no desire to learn further. Even in this age of audiovisual technology and mass media, this is cause for concern.

Information learned from a digest for nothing but the purpose of passing an examination is certainly nothing but knowledge for knowledge's sake. Reading great literature is an opportunity to make connections with the spirits of outstanding writers and in this way to improve and broaden one's self toward further development. Such spiritual improvement comes only from direct contact and cannot be obtained through digests. Although it may be possible to obtain much superficial information without going through the labor of actually reading great books, people who choose this path become spiritually shallow and biased.

Not only in literature but in all other branches of learning as well, educators and students alike must make unceasing and diligent efforts to establish connections between compartmentalized learning and the totality of wisdom. Obviously, abuses in the educational system — like excessive emphasis on examinations — must be corrected. But, even if the system remains imperfect, as long as such efforts are made, students will become people of sufficient ability to transcend its faults. They will go beyond petty egoistic thinking to become total human beings who, while considering the whole of wisdom, relate their own lives to the fate of all humankind. I am firmly convinced that cultivating excellent human beings of this caliber is the true purpose of education.

Creativity: Badge of Humanity

Creativity could be called the badge, or proof, of our humanity. Human beings are the only creatures capable of striving positively and dynamically, day after day, to create newer, higher values.

Creativity is the womb from which individuality blossoms. All humans are different. Each has a unique personality. But often the personality withers in the bud, before it has a chance to come to full flower. In different terms, before coming into individual radiance, personalities frequently freeze at the stage characterized by mere idiosyncrasies. Creativity is a stimulus operating from within to thaw this imbalance and allow the personality to grow and bloom more fully. Buddhism describes the flowering of the personality that emanates from the depths of life with the statement that each person's individuality is as unique as cherry, plum, peach or damson blossoms.

Accordingly, creativity is a brilliant force rising from within. This is what Alfred North Whitehead had in mind when, addressing a group of English students about to leave school in the devastation following World War I, he said that they had all the essential sources of growth within themselves. Knowledge can be obtained from without, but creativity and imagination must be activated from within. Sadly, schools and other institutions of learning today seem to me to fail in stimulating and cultivating creativity.

Young people may be oriented toward good or evil. It is of primary importance for people concerned with education on the broader scale to believe in the creativity of each young person with whom they come in contact, cultivate it warmly, and persistently endeavor to enable it to bloom brilliantly.

I do not deny that abuses in the system — like being absorbed in acquiring the methods to pass examinations — constitute a great barrier to improvement. But it would be irresponsible to lay all the blame at the system's door because exchanges between human beings are the soil in which creativity grows. Creative vitality gushes forth like a fountain as a consequence of spiritual exchanges — sometimes severe, sometimes warm — between human beings who share complete trust given with no thought of reward.

In this connection, I am vividly reminded of a passage in the famous *Epistles* of Plato. About people who claimed to know that which he himself had seriously studied, whether as students of his or of other teachers or from their own discoveries, Plato said, "It is impossible, in my judgment at least, that these men should understand anything about this subject." He then explained, "For it does not at all admit of verbal expression like other studies, but, as a result of continued application to the subject itself and communion herewith, it is brought to the birth in the soul on a sudden, as light that is kindled by a leaping spark, and thereafter it nourishes itself."

In this extremely acute comment, by "this subject," Plato no doubt refers to the quintessence of his own philosophy projected against the background of what he learned under his great teacher Socrates. It is equally certain that the important thing is of a lofty spiritual nature.

His statement that "it is brought to birth in the soul on a sudden, as light that is kindled by a leaping spark, and thereafter it nourishes itself" is an idea widely applicable to modern education. Recognizing each student as a unique personality and transmitting something through contacts between that personality and the personality of the instructor is more than a way of implanting knowledge: it is the essence of education.

In certain parts of Japan, child education is called *ko-yarai*, a term that means allowing the child to stand on his own, out in front, while the parent or educator pushes him from behind. In the words of a Japanese folklorist, this is exactly the opposite of the modern educational tendency to stand in front of the child and attempt to pull him forward. The *ko-yarai* philosophy has something important to say to contemporary educational thought, which considers children less than complete, or mature, human beings until they have completed a prescribed curriculum. Recognition in the field of anthropology of the three elements that modern civilization has overlooked — the primitive, the subconscious and the childlike — is called a great discovery of the twentieth century. Undeniably, education today stands at a turning point in relation to discovering children in the sense of attempting to learn ways to recognize and appreciate the individual personalities of young people.

Educators must make the effort to call forth the creative powers latent in their students. In this undertaking, they require endurance, courage and affection. To cultivate others, an educator must have a glowing, appealing personality. Socrates' power to move others was compared to the shock of a stingray. When told this, Socrates said that the ray stings others because he is himself stung. Similarly, teachers must be constantly creative if they are to evoke creativity from their students. If teachers are not, all their talk of creativity will remain nothing but empty words.

There is nothing wrong with keeping in step with advances in the computer age by introducing all kinds of new equipment to make education more convenient and efficient. But no amount of equipment compensates for the absence of those old, but forever new, virtues of effort, endurance, courage and affection. When these things have dried up, the situation becomes very grave; relying on the latest technology to alleviate it is to put the cart before the horse.

International Outlook

The third element is internationalization. In this age, when the pace of internationalization is accelerating throughout the world, the future of Japan can well be said to depend on the ability to cultivate and foster capable people with truly international perspectives.

For better or worse, Japan has become a world economic leader, and what Japan does has an immense influence on what the world at large does. Dr. Henry Kissinger, with whom I have met on several occasions, says history offers no reason why an economic superpower will not develop into a military superpower. From my own standpoint, however, no matter what history may have been like, to continue to enjoy peace and prosperity, Japan must follow a course other than militarization. And if that path has never before been trodden, Japan must be courageous and take pride in blazing it.

The path I speak of is that of a nation devoted to culture. As an outcome of my many private attempts and undertakings, I have come to see clearly that, whereas it may seem modest and inconspicuous, mutual understanding achieved through cultural exchanges is very powerful.

An episode from the Russo–Japanese War of 1904–1905 is pertinent to this topic. As the war was drawing to a close, Japan was looking about for a nation to serve as mediator. In strict secrecy the Japanese government dispatched two envoys: Kentaro Kaneko, a government official, to the United States and Kentaro Suematsu, a politician and scholar, to England.

Perhaps because the two men had been classmates at Harvard, Kaneko was able to convince President Theodore Roosevelt to assist him. The president, however, asked Kaneko to give him information that would help him explain the Japanese viewpoint to the American people. Kaneko gave Roosevelt a copy of a book, written in English by Inazo Nitobe, called *Bushido, the Spirit of Japan*, in which the code of the warrior is explained as the basis of Japanese moral education. The president read the book in an evening, found it convincing, and agreed to serve as mediator between Japan and Russia.

Suematsu, on the other hand, attended English salons, where he boasted of Japan as a land as much on the way up as the rising sun and was laughed at.

This episode illustrates the way in which culture — like that explained in Nitobe's book — can prove more influential than economic bragging. Unfortunately, after the Russo–Japanese War, Japan pursued a headlong course of militarization. And today, we will find ourselves in a very dangerous predicament unless we strive to make culture the base of our economic power.

To achieve this, the most important thing is to educate people so that they are broadly cultivated and have a mastery of languages. Because this is being realized, Japanese linguistic education, which has in the past been criticized as useless, is now, I am happy to say, being reappraised. I want to make it clear, however, that though an essential element, linguistic proficiency alone does not make a person truly international. As I have said, this requires broad cultivation, not only practical expertise in politics and economics but also an understanding of one's own culture and tradition and those of other peoples as well. The kind of cultivation I have in mind must be so deeply ingrained that it manifests itself in behavior and deportment. As T.S. Eliot says, culture is living. It is not a mere surface accretion but is acquired only when it has been bred into a person since the time of childhood training in manners.

Consequently, a nation devoted to culture must be a nation devoted to education.

The great writer Ogai Mori said: "I divide modern Japanese scholars into those with one and those with two legs. The new Japan is a whirlpool in which the cultures of the East and the West combine. Some scholars stand in the Eastern one and others in the Western one, but both kinds are one-legged.... The age needs scholars with two legs, one planted in each culture. Truly moderate debate is possible only with such people who are the elements of harmony necessary at the present time."

The problem indicated here by Mori, himself a man of great cultivation in Japanese, Chinese and Western cultures, remains unresolved to this day. I think we can expand his meaning of *two-legged* to represent not merely knowledge of the cultures of East and West, but also wide and well-balanced cultivation in general. Today, as internationalization continues to advance, we are in greater need than the people of Mori's time of such "elements of harmony."

In relation to the need for balance and harmony, I should like to mention something that has recently been on my mind. The attitude of the Japanese people toward their own tradition and the traditions of the rest of the world seems to me to have swung, pendulum-like, too wide and too fast in the last fifty years or so. Before World War II, when we were taught that Japan is a divine nation, total rejection of everything un-Japanese was taken for granted. Since World War II, on the other hand, the Japanese tradition — even the best parts of it — has been despised and ignored. Recently, the pendulum seems to be swinging back in the opposite direction again. If this change of attitude is part of an arrogance born of economic success, I am deeply afraid that it could lead Japan in the wrong direction. Rejection and adoration of the foreign are two sides of the same coin, and both indicate a lack of self-confidence and independence. Vacillation and imbalance are the outcome of a lack of self-confidence. People who persist in such a condition can never be called truly international, no matter how much they may pretend to turn their view outward.

Economic and military power can breed arrogance but not self-confidence, which can be fostered only through cultural development. This is why, in Japanese schools, I think it would be a good idea to place more stress on the proper use of the Japanese language and on the study of such aspects of our irreplaceable heritage as great literature and the traditional arts. Without the mature knowledge of one's own language, foreign-language studies cannot produce maximum results. From all that I have seen or heard, people who excel in international contacts are bright and appealing as Japanese personalities. Cultivation in one's own culture as well as in other cultures is what it takes to be truly cosmopolitan; I think our institutions of learning ought to set as one of their goals the development of such internationally minded people.

Although, as I have said, I am no specialist, I have enumerated these three points — totality, creativity and internationalization — because I think a profound understanding of their importance is essential to the reforms that must be made in our current educational system.

10

Perspectives on Virtue

January 26, 1992

In view of the need for a new borderless perspective, it is difficult to be optimistic from where we now stand. Our youth, to whom we will entrust the twenty-first century, look upon neither their future nor their world with bright hope. This is why I feel compelled to discuss the problems of our youth, particularly in the advanced industrialized nations. It is essential that we consider the problems of youth in the wider context of family life.

It is said that children are the mirror of society; young people are quicker than older generations to perceive and respond to the trends of the times. The collapse of socialism in the former Soviet Union and Eastern Europe is significant in this sense. It is no exaggeration to say that, between the Russian Revolution and the fall of the Soviet Union, a period spanning more than half of the twentieth century, socialism virtually monopolized the position as the most ideal system in humankind's history.

Although different countries conceived of it in different ways depending on their developmental stage and geographical location, the socialism of the so-called Red Thirties represented the goal of historical progress and development, and it provided lasting spiritual support to all people who would not tolerate evil and injustice. It was especially appealing to the young, whose hearts burned with idealism. At long last, however, this tendency began to fade in the last quarter of the century, and the final blow came with the sudden collapse of socialist regimes in the former Soviet Union and Eastern Europe in the late 1980s. The young activists of the past, with their outpouring of youthful energy, their indomitable and devoted spirit proudly expressed in the full-voiced singing of "L'Internationale," their eyes alight with idealism, have virtually disappeared from the main stage of world history.

With the realization that, far from being a utopia at the end of the rainbow, their promised land was in fact a wasteland filled with oppression and servitude, the world's youth have been drawn into a whirlpool of confused values. In a way, it is only natural they have fallen under the spell of Mammon and have come to look upon material wealth as the only thing they can trust.

The ostensible "victors" in the Cold War, the countries of the Free World, have not escaped this phenomenon. There, in every corner of society, a desolation is emerging that does not seem in keeping with the glory of victory. The misconduct of youth and the rise of crime are expressions of an underlying malaise. Although there is no end to the list of people who lament our future and sound the alarm, Boston University President John

Silber makes an insightful observation when he says, "The greatest threat lies within our own borders and within each of us." He elaborates as follows:

> We bear the unmistakable traces of self-indulgence. The habits developed through years of ease and plenty have left us, if not at our worst, very far from our best. We seem incapable of making those decisions that, though imperative for our own well-being and that of our children, require unwelcome self-restraint and self-denial. This failure in self-mastery is apparent not only in individual lives but in every aspect of our society. Through self-indulgence and seductive advertising we have turned our luxuries, even our whims, into needs.[1]

There is perhaps nothing new about Dr. Silber's assertions. They were taken from a book that happened to be close at hand and reflect what might be considered common knowledge. The same sentiments can be found in this classic utterance of Rousseau: "Do you know the surest way to make your child miserable? Let him have everything he wants. . . ."[2] As this implies, people in all ages have recognized that the curbing of selfish impulses is the first step in developing good habits, and that freedom without self-restraint leads to self-indulgence, unhappiness, confusion and, in extreme cases, tyranny.

The most serious problem we face is the difficulty of instilling this common knowledge, this reasoning, in the hearts of our youth. Dr. Silber contends that the rising dissatisfaction with hedonism and materialism currently spreading among the American people represents a hopeful sign of sweeping change. While I have great respect for his optimistic conclusion, I do not believe things are really that simple.

I say this because what is really being questioned here is the very principle that has served as the driving force for modern civilization. As we all know, modern industrial civilization places priority on convenience and efficiency as the primary standards of progress and development, and in this context it is difficult to avoid, or indeed resist, the single-minded pursuit of pleasure, which has become the supreme value. Therefore, the materialism, hedonism and mammonism that have clouded the end of this past century are almost the inevitable consequences of modern civilization, which has neglected to rein in human desire. In addition, overwhelming waves of urbanization and information networks generated by technological advancement in industrialized society have enveloped homes, schools and local communities that once provided important educational forums for our youth. In the past, these were the places children were taught discipline, a function severely limited today.

Under these circumstances it is extremely difficult to preach the time-honored virtues of modesty and frugality; in fact, if handled poorly, any attempt to do so can become the stuff of parody, as those in the (broadly defined) teaching profession understand better than anyone. It is not enough to simply decry "negative" aspects of modern civilization such as materialism, hedonism and mammonism. We must also show our youth new standards and values that can take the place of the negative ones and provide them with models to help them become what they need to be: people in control of their own desires and deportment. If the self-restraint and self-control we profess are not based on true conviction, our efforts will not be persuasive, nor can we instill an ethos of world citizenship in the younger generation.

In antiquity, one man placed himself right in the middle of the chaos of his times and resolutely attempted the task of instilling just such an ethos: that great and immortal educator of youth, the "Teacher of Humankind," Socrates. He lived in a time when the democratic government of Athens was in decline, and undoubtedly the confusion of values typical of such an era cast a dark shadow over young hearts. The dialogues of Plato provide ample evidence of this. It was the Sophists — philosophers like Protagoras, Gorgias, Prodicus and Hippias — who controlled the education of the lost young souls buffeted by the currents of their times with no protective harbor; and with that control, they maintained both their wealth and reputations as they pleased.

A typical example of their educational technique can be found in Xenophon's "Memorabilia," where Gorgias speaks about the "Trials of Heracles." Because it constitutes a textbook pattern of moral education common to all times and places, I will quote it here at some length.

When Heracles was on the verge of manhood, he came upon a fork in the road and did not know which to take, at which point two women appeared before him. "The one was fair to see and of high bearing; her limbs were adorned with purity, her eyes with modesty; sober was her figure, and her robe was white. The other was plump and soft, with high feeding. Her face was made up to heighten its natural white and pink, her figure to exaggerate her height."[3] Of course, the former lady was there to lead Heracles toward virtue, and the latter to entice him toward vice.

I will omit what the advocate of evil said, because it is identical to Rousseau's "surest way to make a child miserable." Here are the words of the advocate of virtue: "But I will not deceive you by a pleasant prelude: I will rather tell you truly the things that are, as the gods have ordained them. For of all things good and fair, the gods give nothing to man without toil and effort. If you want the favour of the gods, you must worship the gods: if you desire the love of friends, you must do good to your friends: if you covet honour from a city, you must aid that city: if you fain to win the admiration of all Hellas for virtue, you must strive to do good to Hellas: if you want land to yield you fruits in abundance, you must cultivate that land."[4]

This goes further than Rousseau; in fact, it is a classic pattern for youth education that also underlies Confucian morality and represents a common sense, sound doctrine with which anyone can agree. The loss of awareness that "nothing good and fair" can be won "without toil and effort" is exactly what Dr. Silber so deeply laments in his book.

As I have already mentioned, our problem lies in the fact that present social conditions are far beyond the stage at which we can simply preach this sound doctrine as is and expect it to be accepted. In other words, it is not just a simple matter, for example, of increasing the time spent on moral instruction in our schools. That is not enough. An extremely interesting article on Japanese morality by Professor Masahiko Fujiwara of Ochanomizu Women's University addresses this point. Based on his own experience, Professor Fujiwara focuses on the Japanese "way of the warrior" (Bushido), a code of ethics that has been compared with the English concepts of chivalry and gentlemanly behavior. He strongly felt the need to reassess Bushido as a means of recovering the Japanese ethos that once fascinated the people of the West. When he had his first-year students read Inazo Nitobe's famous work, *Bushido*, however, he found that they rejected it in far stronger terms than he had anticipated. He writes: "For these students, who were steeped in Western individualism, the virtues of loyalty to one's country, filial piety and obligation to the family were nothing more than a joke; in today's materially oriented social climate, the concepts of honor and shame have only secondary importance. Some students even grew indignant at the idea of valuing honor above life, calling the whole notion nonsense."[5]

Given these dominant social norms, it is frighteningly difficult to convince our youth that nothing of value can be obtained "without toil and effort." Not only that, but the adults who espouse such classical moral values are themselves thoroughly immersed in modern civilization, with its emphasis on convenience, efficiency and pleasure. Under the circumstances, we cannot expect young people to accept traditional values as they are. Failing to realize this, any attempt to preach from a position of impertinent moral superiority will only invite apathy and rejection from our youth.

Although we must be wary of facile comparisons, it seems clear that those famous Sophists in Athens also looked down upon their juniors with a supercilious, ostentatiously learned attitude. As Plato so vividly describes, even Protagoras, known for his aphorism that "man is the measure of all things," was tainted by that aura.

Socrates himself trenchantly addressed this point. A single reading of "Protagoras," "Meno" and other dialogues concerned with the education of youth reveals that Socrates concentrates not on the question, "What is virtue?" but rather on the question, "What is not virtue?" Whether it be courage or temperance, justice or piety, not a single established virtue, such as those explicated in Prodicus's "Trials of Heracles," escapes Socrates' piercing examination. And each time the discussion is played out, the foundation for all virtues is razed, and we return to the question of whether moral education is in fact possible. In "Protagoras," we find these lines: "And I should like to work our way back through it until at last we reach what virtue is, and then go back and wonder whether it is teachable or not."[6]

Similarly, in "Meno" we find: "But the certainty of this we shall only know when, before asking in what way virtue comes to mankind, we set about inquiring what virtue is, in and of itself."[7]

I believe we must thoroughly pursue a Socratic examination of virtue, which, in today's society, presents such a wretched, antiquated figure. If virtue is not thrust into the furnace and cast anew, it cannot be reborn as a new ethical standard. Without this, no amount of energetic exhortation will avail us; the bewilderment and unreceptiveness of our youth will go uncorrected, and we will suffer an ever-widening gap between generations.

The questions of what virtue meant to Socrates and whether he thought moral education was possible, involve the subtle philosophical concepts of "idea" and "*mutos*" (myth). Setting such finer points aside, we must note that the most important thing from the educational point of view is that the Socratic approach, of examining what does not constitute virtue, was far more persuasive and instilled a far more lasting impression in the hearts of students than the Sophist emphasis on examining what does constitute virtue. This is clearly demonstrated by the fact that the authorities, who feared Socrates' influence, decreed his death to ensure his silence.

But where did this rare persuasiveness, this uncommon influence, originate? It arose because Socrates was more acutely aware of his era than anyone else. He scrutinized it more keenly and deeply; and more than anyone else, he lived through his time with full vigor, ready to sacrifice his own life. The attractiveness of his lifestyle, the magnetism that emanated from his very humanity, could not but reach the impressionable hearts of the young. Regardless of the times, there lies unchanging in the depths of the young human soul an earnestness that responds to earnestness, a seriousness that reacts to seriousness; this is the true character and prerogative of youth. In his reply to Meno, who likened Socrates to the torpedo that paralyzes anyone who comes in touch with it, Socrates said: "As for me, if the torpedo is torpid itself, while causing others to be torpid, I am like it, but not otherwise."[8]

I believe this is the ironclad principle — indeed, the imperishable "golden rule" of human education and moral upbringing: that the fervent involvement of the teacher is precisely what gets the students involved. In this there is no trace of contemptuousness in the teacher's attitude toward those who are learning; rather the relationship is maintained on a thoroughly equal and fair basis. Reverberating from such a relationship is the resonance of individual personalities associating and interacting in earnest and in harmony as complete human beings. The form of trust created in this way is precisely what has been called "virtue" since antiquity. It seems to me that this is where we must seek the underlying, fundamental cause for the rising misbehavior, crime and other problems we observe among modern youth: the lack of fully human interaction between individuals. We cannot expect our various treatments for the symptoms of this "disease" to work effectively at least until we clearly address this underlying need.

In his *Essays*, Montaigne wrote: "Someone asked Socrates of what country he was. He did not answer, 'Of Athens,' but 'Of the world.' He, whose imagination was fuller and wider, embraced the whole world as his city, and extended his acquaintance."[9]

The goal of the SGI movement is nothing less than this: to instill an ethos of worldwide citizenry. As it was with Socrates, so it shall be for us: by defining ourselves as citizens of the world, we can revitalize the now almost faded virtues of courage, self-control, devotion, justice, love and friendship, and make them vibrantly pulse in people's hearts. That is why, in my comments for the 1991 SGI Day (January 26), I observed: "If a religion is worthy of the name, and if it is one that can respond to the needs of contemporary times, it should be able to nurture in its followers the spiritual base for becoming good citizens of the world." I went on to suggest that, rather than attempt unprincipled compromise or collusion among different religions, we should instead encourage them to compete in the task of producing world citizens.

11

A True Restoration of Humanity

Entrance Ceremony of Soka University,
Tokyo, April 9, 1973

This university belongs to all of you. It must not be an ivory tower, isolated from society. Instead, it must be a tower of hope with boundless possibilities for the unfolding of a new era in history. I want you to adopt this attitude toward the university and to bear in mind always the need to devote thought and effort to doing whatever you can for the happiness of humanity.

Today, let us examine the influence the university has exerted on society from the historical viewpoint. I do not intend to delve into an abstruse, abstract theory of the role of the university. I am not qualified to make such a talk nor is there any need for one. I intend only to give a few examples of the ways in which the university — or, on the broader scale, learning in general — has been a compelling force in history.

Emergence of the University in the West

All of you are familiar with the cultural awakening that took place in the fourteenth and fifteenth centuries in Europe called the Renaissance. This was a time when the long-dormant spirit of humanism awakened to inspire in painting, sculpture, literature and the other arts a long series of works glorifying the human being. Europe was then greeting a new dawn. I am certain I am not the only person who senses a crystallization of human joy in the artistic creations of the Renaissance.

This important epoch in European history was no mere accidental revolution in art and literature. The way had been prepared by a quickening that arose from the depths of European culture. This quickening took the form of a revival of learning during the twelfth century, which, though less well known, was actually just as important as the Renaissance of the fourteenth and fifteenth centuries. Historians sensitive to its value call this movement the Renaissance of the Twelfth Century. During this period the European style university came into being.

In the Middle Ages, higher education was limited to the seven so-called liberal arts — Latin grammar, rhetoric, logic, arithmetic, astronomy, geometry and music. These were considered necessary to the reading of the Bible for an understanding of God's natural laws and for the management of common law to support regal authority. Arithmetic and astronomy were needed for calculating church history, and music for church rituals. The other branches of learning were applied in law and politics.

In about the twelfth century, to these studies were added — especially in Spain and Italy — mathematics, philosophy, geography and law, all of which were imported from the Islamic world. Among these imports were subjects that had been known to the ancient Greeks and Romans but that had been forgotten in medieval Europe. Other elements had been brought by Muslims and Italian merchants from India and the East. With the acquisition of this heritage of ancient — though new to Europe — learning, there took place an irrepressible drive to absorb still more, newer knowledge and to accumulate and systematize it.

Young people in search of knowledge broke from the bonds of the monastic schools and sought new repositories of learning. It might be said that the educational profession arose in response to their demands, with the formation in Paris and Bologna of organized bodies of teachers and students. This formation constituted the emergence of the European university.

The word *university* derives from the Latin *universitas*, one of the meanings of which is a society or guild, or a number of people in a group. In other words, the university is basically a united group of teachers and students, not necessarily buildings or an educational system. It began with connections among people. The university at Paris originated largely for research and reorganization of theology. The university at Bologna concentrated on law. Both institutions were sources of revised thought on traditional ecclesiasticism and were the scenes of increased modern, rational learning and knowledge, which was to be applied in rules governing the new kind of commercial transactions developing at the time.

The Need for a Profound Philosophical Heritage

The spiritual core of the quest for learning was humanism. I believe that the growth of the bourgeoisie and the increased vigor of commerce made possible the development of an intellectual class outside the framework of the aristocracy and topped by the university. This class created the ripe opportunity for the Renaissance. A steady examination of the human condition, combined with a desire for learning in search of truth, gradually stimulated a revival of the arts, which became a paean to humankind. The Renaissance could not have altered the course of history if it had been merely a shallow movement in literature and the arts. It was epoch-making because it rested on human self-awareness, freed from the restraints of the older society and endorsed by profound scholarly assurance.

The work of Leonardo da Vinci reveals the effect of the new learning. The perspective he employs in his painting is based on knowledge of geometry, and the study of anatomy and actual dissections gave him information for his delicate drawings of human beings and animals.

Reflecting on the influence of the twelfth century, we can see that the accumulation of learning and knowledge since that time made possible the brilliant works we attribute to the Renaissance. The point I want to make is this: The elements that have the power to influence history result from human thought and the tide of life. To flourish, grow and have wide effect, a civilization requires a profound philosophical heritage at its base. Without such a heritage, a civilization cannot produce geniuses. And, even if it could produce them, the geniuses would find no place to manifest their talents. Furthermore, a social structure built on the ethic of power alone cannot influence human life deeply or leave a brilliant historical record.

People often tend to grasp only the glorious, superficial products of history. They copy styles, respect established traditions and attempt to use them as basic principles of action, while ignoring the deeper causes that made possible the achievement of such glories. I believe the failure to look more deeply into historical phenomena explains the failure of past attempts at reformation. Action that exists for nothing but the attainment of the immediate goal must ultimately be idle and futile.

The University as a Basic Current of Civilization

The university is a repository of intellectual heritage. The quality and significance of the research and education carried out there can determine the fate of a nation, a society or an entire civilization. Where learning flourishes, the people flourish. The ancient civilizations demonstrate the truth of these statements. At its peak, the world of Islam had many centers of learning, as did India in the heyday of Buddhism. The ancient Indian Buddhist university of Nalanda, which had an area of tens of square kilometers, dates back more than twelve hundred years. It reached its zenith between the fifth and seventh centuries. Larger in scale than most modern universities and much older than the universities of Europe, Nalanda was a spiritual center for both India and the whole Orient. Many Chinese students are known to have gone there to study. Uncovering several study rooms and dormitory rooms, recent excavations made it clear that, at one time, Nalanda could have accommodated as many as ten thousand students. The Chinese priest Hsuan Tsang, who visited Nalanda, recorded his impressions in the *Great T'ang Record of Western Countries*. Excavations have unexpectedly verified the material in this book. Nalanda developed and propagated the principles of Mahayana Buddhism for centuries, until it was destroyed by invading Muslims.

It is possible to trace the current of influence of this university in the great flow of Buddhist teachings from India to China and then to Japan. Recalling the thousands of Buddhist priests who once earnestly discussed Buddhism, debated important points and then took what they had learned back to their home countries for practical application, I am convinced that Nalanda must indeed have been a fountainhead of Oriental spiritual culture worthy of the respect of the whole world.

Ancient Seats of Learning Based on Humanism

Respect for humanity must be the basis of all institutions of learning. I have already shown that humanism was the foundation of the universities of the Renaissance, but something similar can also be said of more ancient institutions of learning that cannot accurately be described as universities in the modern sense. Plato's Akademeia in the grove of Akadomos is a case in point. In the Athens of his time, the Sophists acquired considerable influence through their rhetoric and their professional, purely pragmatic approach to teaching — they imparted to students only such knowledge as was needed to get ahead in the world. Socrates, who advocated the search for truth as the ideal, opposed the Sophists. Confronting the sunset of the Grecian world, he attempted to reform Athens on the basis of a philosophy devoted to understanding the truth about human nature. For this reason, he took a stand against philosophers who taught only pragmatism and reliance on systems. Furthermore, he devoted himself to a learning that would remain valid eternally. For Socrates, the market, the street corner, the banquet or any of the places human beings gathered were proper places for transmitting his beliefs to young people and combating what he considered to be corrupt teaching practices. He conducted true dialogues and training in what amounted to a university without school buildings.

Inheriting the basic beliefs of Socrates, Plato established his Akademeia. Though he employed a definite locale, the education he conducted there was of the humanistic kind that Socrates had favored. In Plato's day, it was customary in Athens to take mealtime as an opportunity for discussing various affairs. Plato followed this practice in teaching. In addition, he conducted lively symposiums on philosophical and humanistic subjects during strolls with his students.

The attitude reflected in dialogues between students and teachers can be seen in the search for truth conducted by Plato and his followers. It was the pride of the Akademeia that teacher and student together strove to attain one truth. Though entrance requirements were strict, and even though it included certain aristocratic elements, the institution rested on a foundation of faith in freedom and a desire to reform society through philosophy. Men and women studied together, and the school was vigilant against any attempts by secular authority to encroach on its academic freedom. Established around 400 BCE and in operation — until it was finally closed by a Roman emperor — for approximately nine centuries, the Akademeia was a major force in Western spiritual education and, through its methods of dialogue and cooperative search for truth, had a great influence on history.

The teaching method of Shakyamuni, the first historical Buddha, is a still older example of the thorough application of dialogue. Shakyamuni employed questions and answers to impart to others the content of his enlightenment about the fundamental laws governing humanity and the entire universe. Almost all of the sutras are written in a dialogue form in which Shakyamuni comes into direct contact with human suffering and reveals the truth about his own enlightenment. In later times, vast amounts of Buddhist doctrinal material were compiled, but it must be borne in mind always that human contact leading to refinement of the moral character and the search for truth lies at the basis of it all.

The Renaissance plea for a return to the learning of Greece reveals something about the great influence of Plato's Akademeia. In a similar manner, Shakyamuni's humanistic teachings have left an imprint on virtually all of Asian history. I believe that the basic power to exert such an influence is found in one primary aim: to base all efforts in the search for truth on humanity and to elucidate basic human nature so as to inspire moral refinement. Any learning or search for truth that does not have humanistic roots is doomed to be abstract, futile, shallow and fruitless.

At present the world stands in danger of losing sight of the basic elements of human nature.

Increased Spiritual Freedom

Having made these remarks about the nature of the university, I make the following request of you: strive to be creative. The name of this institution — Soka University — means a university for the creation of values. This in turn means that the basic aim of our university is the creation of the wholesome values needed by society. Such values must be either offered to or returned to society. Consequently, all students here must cultivate their creative abilities in the effort to make contributions to a richer future.

A mere bright idea is not necessarily creative. But the production of even bright ideas requires a fairly firm foundation of basic knowledge. Creative work in the fields of scholarship and learning is much more demanding. It is like a mountain pinnacle: it cannot exist without a broad, deep, firm foundation.

The university is the suitable place for the evolution of such a foundation. Unfortunately, though most universities today are blessed with conditions enabling them to do so, they generally overlook the need to direct learning toward the ultimate goal of creative activity. They are not places where people are trained to have creative personalities. I want Soka University to be different. I want it to become an institution brimming with creative vitality, and I want it to introduce fresh air into society.

The spiritual soil must be rich for the cultivation of creativity. This means that spiritual freedom is essential. Independent thought and creative work are impossible under conditions of oppression or distortion. Inexhaustible creative thinking is possible only when the spirit is free to roam over a wide field.

But spiritual freedom does not mean spiritual license. True development can take place only in the presence of both expansive liberty and high-level self-discipline. Spiritual freedom does not give one the right to think and act completely as he or she wishes. My interpretation of true spiritual freedom is the opportunity to grow by means of dialogue to an expanded field of vision and ultimately to an elevated insight in the nature of things. Both in Plato's Akademeia and in the ancient Buddhist university at Nalanda, there was freedom. But there was also stern confrontation with the truth. There was creative thought. And, precisely for these reasons, the Akademeia and Nalanda evolved rich spiritual heritages.

In short, to increase spiritual freedom, strict training is required. Both Oxford and Cambridge are private universities where much has been achieved in the field of learning and where many famous and important scholars have been trained. In both schools, a strict educational system is followed now as in the Middle Ages. But, in both cases, students are given a high degree of freedom to expand spiritually and to prepare themselves to make their contributions to society.

What is the source of the energy that enables humanity to increase its spiritual freedom and broaden its range of activities? In asking this question, I inevitably return to the more fundamental issue of the true nature of humanity and to the philosophy that brings forth, develops and elevates latent human talents.

Please remember that all the educational institutions I have mentioned had a backbone of humanistic educational philosophy. Free development of learning and rich cultural flowerings arise from a direct contemplation of and an attempt to develop life and humanity. I am convinced this is the key to creativity. I hope Soka University will always aim for the perfection of humanistic learning and for high scholastic achievement. I want all of you to advance in your studies and in the search for truth, so that you can become sources of power in a great reformation of society. I propose that you determine to become creative human beings worthy of the name of Soka (Value-creating) University. If this kind of determination can elevate its already fine tradition, I am convinced that Soka University can become an important, refreshing element in the modern world of Japanese university education, which is now in a state of chaos.

Pride and Devotion

To change the subject slightly, it is my honor to have shared enthusiastic discussions with the famous historian Arnold J. Toynbee on a wide range of topics, including history, philosophy, art, science and education. At our first meeting, I was surprised by the way Mr. Toynbee and his wife greeted me. He said, "I am grateful that you have visited my alma mater, Oxford." And she said, "I am grateful that you have visited my alma mater, Cambridge." It is true that I visited England at the invitations of these two universities. But I had not expected to hear such initial words from Mr. and Mrs. Toynbee. Their greetings, however, showed me how much pride and devotion they felt in Oxford and Cambridge.

In Japan, national universities are frequently more prestigious than private ones; but in Europe and the United States, the opposite is often the case, as is illustrated by Oxford, Cambridge and Harvard, all of which are private institutions. The graduates of such schools are usually very proud of and devoted to their alma maters. When they succeed in their careers, they contribute sizable sums to their universities, which are thereby enabled to improve facilities and services. Please do not worry; I am not saying that you must hurry to become famous so that you can make contributions to Soka University.

Even though as institutions of learning they have a public role to play, private universities are unrelated to national authority. Fundamentally independent, they may seek to train people and make educational achievements toward realizing their own articles of faith. Because they are autonomous, private universities are the product of the action of all the people who operate and study at them. In this sense, they differ from government or state public schools. The very concept of the university began with private institutions. The university emerged spontaneously and was not created to be the servant of governmental needs.

I want all of you to play your parts in the creation and perfection of Soka University. Do not think of your education here as the mere accumulation of learning. Do not regard the university as a passport to a good job. As long as you are here, engage in lively dialogues with your teachers and help evolve a university that is vibrant and warm. You have much to do in this creative building process, since Soka University is new and its traditions and teaching styles are not yet firmly established. I shall be observing what you do and shall always be ready to offer whatever assistance I can.

A New Restoration

In a sense, modern civilization has reached a turning point. Can humanity survive? This is the ominous question facing us. The threat of armaments to peace and a mistaken faith in progress seem to be propelling humanity forward in a march to death. What should we do — what can we do — to enable humankind to survive? Enlightened scholars now debate this issue assiduously.

I cry out that what we need in such a time is another true restoration of humanity. I do not mean human beings are the center of the universe or in any way omnipotent. The restoration I have in mind must enable human beings to live in harmony with all of our other fellow living creatures. People must cease being the servants of machines and must once again be the servants of human beings. The restoration I have in mind would help us find a way to achieve this.

It must be a neo-renaissance, requiring concurrent, immediate renaissance in the fields of philosophy and learning. Without doubt if human beings devote attention to a new desire for learning and take a farsighted view of their condition, a new philosophy enabling humanity to survive will be forthcoming.

Such a philosophy will not only fulfill the negative role of permitting survival but will also sponsor the building of a new civilization that can be a paean to humanity. Soka University will have fulfilled its purpose if it can contribute substantially to the attainment of this goal.

The task is not an easy one. Definite conclusions cannot be reached in a short time. Clearly, the creation of this new civilization demands persevering, repeated, strict debates and determination over a long time. But if all the people associated with Soka University now and all those who will be associated with it in the future — who will no doubt share our thoughts on this point — will cooperate in a single-minded effort, our goal can be achieved. Live a rich, full student life, not only as representatives of this institution but also as its honored founders and creators. Let your experiences here serve as a springboard to a richer life after graduation.

From now on, education will be my major work, for I want to lay firm foundations in this field for the three decades following my death. Leading the people of the twenty-first century to peace and happiness is my sole concern. Because I feel this way, I request that you accept responsibility for the future of humankind. From the bottom of my heart, I ask the members of our faculty to do all within their power to make fine human beings of our students. I shall conclude my remarks by expressing my hope for and pride in the part that Soka University will play in the future of humanity.

12

The Fight To Live a Creative Life

Entrance Ceremony of Soka University,
Tokyo, April 18, 1974

A university is not the result of a system or a building program but a product of the determination and passion of young people seeking new knowledge and wisdom. First of all, determined young people must aspire to make truth their own. To help fulfill such aspirations, teachers and instructors will be found; and, through the cooperative effort of students and instructors, universities will evolve. Fundamentally, the university begins with a thirst for knowledge and a love of truth on the part of the students. The atmosphere of such thirst and love must prevail. A university without eager students is a university without life, a university in which the main purpose has been forgotten. The time has come to return to the true origins of university education.

During a discussion of the gap between professors and students, a leading professor at San Marcos University brought up two interesting points. First, he said that the dialogue between students and professors must always continue. Second, the university must always permit students to take a responsible part in general affairs and activities. Searching for the proper direction in which to lead his university, he perceived the importance of giving students the leading role, and he was trying to find new solutions suited to the trends of our time. Here at Soka University, you must not wait passively for the university to do something for you but must join proudly, bravely, actively, passionately in making this university a new light of hope. Dialogue must continue, but it must be useful and profitable and based on responsibility and trust, not irresponsible arguments. This is your university. You are responsible for it. Remember that we are all united in wanting to make Soka University a springboard for the advancement of human culture. If you remember these things, your dialogues will be fruitful. We must create at this university a magnificent community of human beings joined together in a common cause.

The Special Nature of Private Universities.
Fundamentally, the purpose of private universities is to create an opportunity for the free, spontaneous pursuit of knowledge, unhampered by government controls. In a free university, it is possible to develop human beings capable of considering the future of humankind as a whole and of maintaining a universal viewpoint. It is the special function of a private university to send out into the world young people free of narrow nationalism or racial contentiousness, who can think broadly enough

to act on a world-encompassing stage, and who can work for a revolution in our troubled and hectic society.

Like all other institutions of higher learning, private universities must be devoted to scholarship and research; but a private university should always have a liberal, lively atmosphere, completely free from the clannishness of scholarly cliques. The special mission of the private university is to maintain conditions under which there is always absolute freedom of thought, freedom of study and freedom of publication. An institute of learning founded on such freedoms will invariably foster independent research and yield scholars rich in individuality and creativity. It is the duty of a private university to avoid being caught up in evanescent trends and to sponsor long-range research of the widest possible scope.

The education and research of which I have been speaking have been the true goals of the university system ever since the first such institution was founded. Unfortunately, for all their undeniable good features, government universities can never ignore the demands or limitations imposed on them from above.

While meeting the needs of its own country or that country's people, the private university is free to look beyond to world needs in general. The private university must be a stronghold, resisting interference from government authorities and offering firm protection to true learning and culture.

Since the late nineteenth century, Japan's custom has been to regard government schools, and particularly national or prefectural universities, as the main sources of youth education and cultural enlightenment. Not only among educators but among many other people as well, government universities are thought to represent the mainstream of education. As I consider the future of Japan and the rest of the world, however, it seems to me that, if the spirit of the university is to be a living force in society, we must reverse this situation and find the mainstream of education in private universities.

Today we need bright young people who have studied at private universities to acquire not only knowledge and wisdom but also freedom and independence of thought. When such young people travel about the world, working or relaxing with the masses of humanity, we will begin to have a new kind of cultural exchange and fusion among individuals and peoples. We will, in short, have cultural interchange at the grass-roots level, instead of only among diplomats and the elite. The day will come when cultural bridges will link the peoples of the earth, when friendships will stretch across all national barriers, when people's hearts will respond joyfully to the birth peal of a new global culture and a new civilization for all humankind. You must become the envoys and the builders of the bridges of culture and peace connecting the peoples of the world. You must toll the great bell announcing to future generations the birth of a new global culture. The reverberations of that bell will echo the yearnings of multitudes of people in all nations.

Power and Wisdom

Recently the French social scientist Georges Friedmann, noted for his research on labor movements, published a book called *The Power and the Wisdom*. The word *power* in the title refers to human power to control the environment by scientific or technological means. *Wisdom* means to him the intelligence to harness this power and use it creatively for the welfare of humanity. Though I do not intend to explain the contents of Friedmann's book, I should like to make use of his distinction between power and wisdom.

From the late nineteenth and early twentieth centuries until the end of World War II, Japanese education, particularly college education, was all too strongly oriented toward acquisition of power. Its purpose was to absorb knowledge, master various techniques and bring Japan up to the same level of power as America and the nations of Europe. After long years of seclusion, Japan lagged far behind the Western nations in science; and there was a real fear that, without power, acquired as quickly as possible, it might be colonized and trampled upon by other countries. By virtue of the so-called rich country, strong army policy, Japan did manage to maintain her independence, while other countries of Asia were, one by one, being deprived of theirs. In the long run, however, excessive emphasis on power and continued pursuit of the "rich country, strong army" policy resulted in an unprecedented defeat in war.

Regarded as a means to attain power, prewar education lacked the respect for human beings that is ultimately the lifeblood of learning and failed to inculcate in young people a sense of the dignity of human life. Instead, it strove to produce people valuable to the nation or industry, people who were mere cogs in government or industrial organizations. Education was the means whereby this end product was achieved.

It is important to acquire power, but the acquisition of power must always be accompanied by the development of wisdom. Wisdom is rooted in the souls of human beings. The way to acquire it is to follow the simple advice of Socrates: "Know thyself." This is the starting point for establishing a sense of human dignity, preventing the degradation of human beings into anonymous, interchangeable machine cogs. The essence of true knowledge is self-knowledge. This is the ideal of education and learning at Soka University. Countless splendid universities and research institutions in the world can give power. But what have they done for humanity? The cruel emptiness and frustration of contemporary civilization are the outcomes of their kind of education.

Your mission is to acquire the wisdom that will enable you to use power for the happiness and peace of humanity. Know yourselves and, armed with that knowledge, study. Think of things in relation to yourselves as human beings, reexamine the meaning of knowledge, science and art to humanity, for such inquiry can lead to a new revival of humankind. I am certain that if we accumulate both power and wisdom, eventually a great Renaissance will take place in human culture.

The French art historian René Huyghe gave a lecture at Tokyo University titled "Form and Strength," as related to nature and art. At one point he said: "The crisis of our times is a crisis of civilization, the danger of materialism carried too far. The failing of our culture is compartmentalization of everything and failure to keep sight of the whole. I believe that human civilization is a single, indivisible entity and that intellectuals must use their knowledge and power on behalf of civilization. The crisis we face today is not merely a social or political crisis, but a fundamental crisis of civilization."

Open the Door

Allow me to elaborate, today, on what we mean by a creative life. I am not about to launch forth upon a difficult philosophical disquisition or try to give you a definitive explanation of life. I merely urge you to become cheerful travelers on life's long road. Let me suggest something from my own experience that may help bring honor and glory to your future.

I feel most deeply that I have done something creative when I have thrown myself wholeheartedly into a task and fought it through unstintingly to its conclusion and thus have won in the struggle to enlarge myself. It is a matter of sweat and tears. The creative life demands constant effort to improve one's thoughts and actions. Perhaps the dynamism involved in effort is the important thing.

You will pass through storms, and you may suffer defeat. The essence of the creative life, however, is to persevere in the face of defeat and to follow the rainbow within your heart. Indulgence and indolence are not creative. Complaints and evasions are cowardly, and they corrupt life's natural tendency toward creation. The person who gives up the fight for creativeness is headed ultimately for the hell that destroys all life.

You must never slacken in your efforts to build new lives for yourselves. Creativeness means pushing open the heavy door to life. This is not an easy struggle. Indeed, it may be the hardest task in the world. For opening the door to your own life is more difficult than opening the doors to the mysteries of the universe.

But the act of opening your door vindicates your existence as a human being and makes life worth living. None are lonelier or unhappier than those who do not know the pure joy of creating a life for themselves. To be human is not merely to stand erect and manifest reason and intellect: to be human in the full sense of the word is to lead a creative life.

The fight to create a new life is a truly wonderful thing, revealing radiant wisdom, the light of intuition that leads to an understanding of the universe, the strong will of justice and a determination to challenge all attacking evils, the compassion that enables you to take upon yourself the sorrows of others, and a sense of union with the energy of compassion gushing forth from the cosmic source of life and creating an ecstatic rhythm in the lives of all human beings. As you challenge adversity and polish the jewel that is life, you will learn to walk the supreme pathway of true humanity. Whoever leads a creative life from the present into the future will stand in the vanguard of history. I think of this flowering of the creative life as the human revolution that is your mission now and throughout your lives.

The nineteenth-century French poet and writer Charles Péguy said: "The crisis of education is not a crisis of education but a crisis of life." The crisis we face today strikes at the very roots of education and learning. And yet it is in education and learning that we will find the doorway to the future.

PART TWO

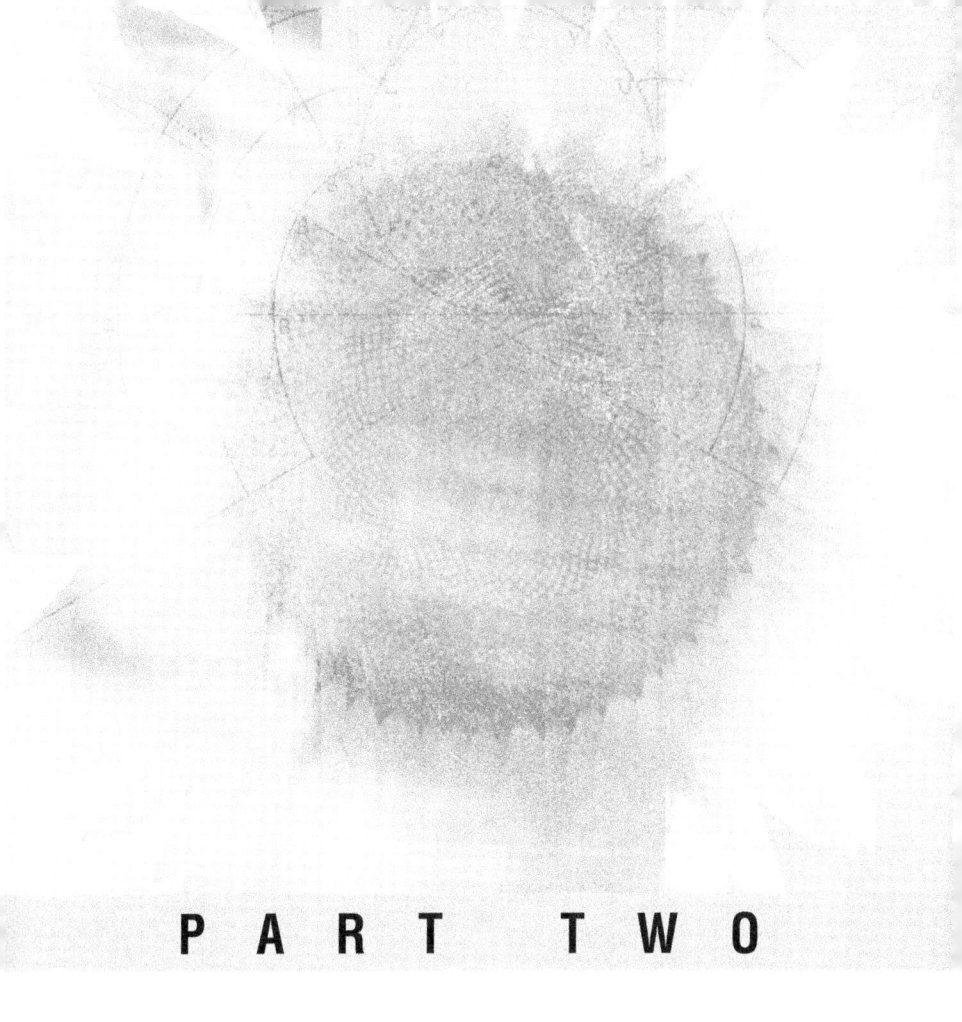

Brief Thoughts

Excerpts on Education

- Only a human being can foster another human being. It takes a truly humanistic person to raise a truly humanistic person. Schoolteachers and others dedicated to developing people carry out a task of immeasurable value. The effects of this task will last forever.

- Youth is power. To bring out the best in young people and to fuel their strength are the role of education, thereby promoting their growth. Youth should shoulder the future; there is no way to create a greater future than with our present commitment to education.

- Education, based on open dialogue, is far more than the mere transfer of information and knowledge; it enables us to rise above the confines of our parochial perspectives and passions.

- Education is a weapon to liberate humankind and rid our world of the human suffering caused by ignorance and other societal ills.

- Long before the outbreak of World War II, first Soka Gakkai president Tsunesaburo Makiguchi advocated and was instrumental in implementing numerous innovative reforms in the field of education. To list a few examples, he proposed such things as promoting education in outlying regions, a half-day school system, government-funded school lunches, and education at special elementary schools for children of the poor. Later, many of these proposals were incorporated, bit by bit, into Japan's postwar educational reforms. One of Mr. Makiguchi's particular concerns was securing the autonomy of education. This is a very important point.

- In discussing the merits of value-creating education, Mr. Makiguchi advocated helping children develop the ability to chart, and advance upon, their own chosen course, whether it be in a certain discipline or in life. He expressed a repugnance for cramming children's heads with knowledge of little practical value. Value-creating education, he asserted, means to cultivate the ability to create benefit and remove harm, to emphasize good and avoid evil, to create beauty and cast off the ugly, while at the same time being responsive to all environments. He slammed the type of education that lays a disproportionate emphasis on intellectual training and rote-learning. A knowledgeable or intellectual person is not necessarily a wise person. Knowledge, however abundant it may be, is wasted unless it is put to practical use. Indeed there are many people who, though possessing highly specialized knowledge, lack good common sense. Those who actively create the values of beauty, benefit and good wherever they are and in whatever circumstances they find themselves are people of wisdom. Polishing and acquiring this kind of wisdom is the meaning of value creation (*soka*).

- President Makiguchi wrote *The Geography of Human Life* when he was thirty-two. What is the underlying theme that he pursues throughout this great work of his youth? In short, it is the desire to develop open-minded human beings; it is nothing less than his conviction that one must adhere unwaveringly to the path of humanism. Thus, President Makiguchi waged a difficult struggle against the characteristic insularity of Japan — an island-country that had for centuries maintained a self-imposed isolation from the rest of the world. He blamed this insularity for the production of closed-minded human beings.

- Mr. Makiguchi once said: "Teachers must not instruct students with the arrogant attitude of 'Become like me!' It is far more important for teachers to adopt the attitude, 'Don't satisfy yourself with trying to become like me. Make your model someone of higher caliber.' True teachers [who are genuinely concerned for the development of each student], therefore, are those who have the humility to advance together with their students. Education must never be coercive. The heart of education lies in the process of teacher and pupil learning together, the teacher drawing forth the pupil's potential and raising the pupil to surpass the teacher in ability."

- In his work, *The System of Value-Creating Pedagogy*, Mr. Makiguchi insists that education is the key, the spring from which a spiritual rebirth and the realization of utopia would flow. He identified education as the universal hope of humankind. Religion without education leads to the deception and exploitation of the people by the clergy. To truly make the most of religion, it is imperative that people first become wise and strong.

- The origin of Mr. Makiguchi's philosophy of education was the educator's strong desire to make all of the children at his elementary school happy.

- Mr. Makiguchi long studied the differences between the type of person whose presence is desired by everyone with the type of person whose presence is a source of trouble. He observed that the kind of people one wants to have around are those who can think beyond their own personal gain and focus on contributing to society as a whole. As a result, the societal value of those who possess this type of character will be recognized by the vast majority. Such individuals will be praised and respected for their achievements. The cultivation of this sort of character value is the aim of Soka education.

- The university is a fortress where, led by the light of reason, human beings achieve spiritual development; it is also a castle for defending civilization against barbarism, a castle founded on the love of truth. A university no doubt is in the vanguard of the effort to expel ignorance — the basic cause for all miseries — from the earth. Because we have founded a university we have participated in the creation of a future. A university in the present is the epitome of society in the future. Therefore, please be convinced that the success of our university will contribute to the triumph of humankind.

- A university's mission is not to produce people of authority but people of true ability, intelligence and conviction who will dedicate themselves to the good of the people. Can universities raise and send individuals into society capable of shouldering the next age? The answer to this vital question will determine not only the victory or defeat of the academic world but the destiny of the age as well.

- How do we prove a university's worth? It is alive in its graduates. We must look to the activities in society of those who studied and were nurtured at a university. They are a clear mirror of the true substance of the university. In that sense, our graduates are a sort of living Soka University. As the scope of their activities expands, the possibilities for those who come after them expand as well. In larger social terms, the road to building a peaceful society is also opened. And that represents the further development of Soka University.

- The university exists for the sake of the students. We must permit no one to take their freedom or dignity away. Faculty members, too, must put the concerns of the students first in all areas. They must respect and treasure the students as comrades and equals. This is the fundamental spirit of Soka University.

- Institutes of higher learning are charged with the task of encouraging Socratic world citizens and spearheading the search for new principles for the peaceful integration of our world.

- What the world urgently needs now is an age of wisdom. No matter how much information or knowledge we may have, it does not necessarily produce value or bring happiness. The power of wisdom effectively puts that knowledge and information to use, puts them into action.

- Josei Toda (second president of the Soka Gakkai) once advised us: "Those who put the highest priority on fame and wealth lack the qualification to be leaders in the truest sense. The same applies to educators. Students, with their sensitive minds, can immediately and clearly discern the egoism of teachers. Only pure and lofty passion within a person who has become free from mundane desires can penetrate the pure hearts of students, evoking a response of sympathy and attentiveness."

- During Josei Toda's first meeting with his predecessor, Tsunesaburo Makiguchi, Mr. Toda expressed his deep passion for education: "I am confident that I can transform even the most incapable student into an outstanding one. Education, or the fostering of capable people, is indeed a noble mission, and those with a deep sense of responsibility who completely dedicate themselves to this mission are truly worthy of respect."

- The level of culture that teachers have attained in the depths of their lives through their own personal effort is conveyed from one human being to another, from teacher to student. Education is not something conferred in a highhanded manner from without. Consequently, teachers' inner growth contributes to students' happiness and educational and social advances.

- The virtue of sincerity is the foundation of a praiseworthy life, and it should also be the basis of education.

- Efforts to instill confidence and trust in students are more important than the institution or the methodology. Maintaining a sincere and serious attitude to give every possible consideration to the students should be the teacher's primary concern. School doesn't exist for the teachers but for the students.

- It is essential to create an environment in which students can discover the joys of learning and inquiring into the world around them. The teacher could be considered the greatest influence, or "environmental factor," in a student's education, because the teacher's attitude and character have a decisive impact on the growth and development of those being taught. Teachers must recognize the good points of each student and wholeheartedly praise any efforts the student makes in order to further bring forth his or her potential.

- Young people are sensitive. It is cruel to make comparisons among them. It is foolish. Cherry blossoms are cherry blossoms, and plum blossoms are plum blossoms. Students should be shown warm compassion, so they can grow at their own rate and in a way true to themselves.

- Our smallest efforts can make a big difference in a child's education. Let us take care not to ignore children but to talk to them and tell them about things, however small, as they really are. It's important to speak to children as we would another adult. Even if they don't understand completely now, someday the seed we plant will sprout.

- Youth is the time for building one's foundation in life. You cannot expect to build a great hall or high-rise building without first setting a solid and secure foundation. In the same way, you cannot realize a glorious future in life if you neglect earnest study or shy away from hard work. Everything depends on the extent to which you train and polish yourself. If, content with summary knowledge and strategies, you avoid the efforts that building a foundation entails, you will later experience loss.

- Anything significant can be improved and even perfected through repeated effort. If students are to pass difficult exams, they must challenge themselves, studying day in and day out. The correct attitude in life is accumulating efforts and advancing steadily.

- Knowledge must be fully absorbed; you must make it a part of yourselves. In that effort, you must develop your own wisdom. You cannot attain wisdom without first walking through the door of knowledge. On the other hand, unless you acquire wisdom, you will drown in a flood of knowledge and lose sight of the right direction in life.

- Those who may be considered truly well-educated people possess their own clear system of values, their own clear beliefs and opinions, not borrowed from someone else. They base their lives on their own firm convictions, and they do not simply follow convention. They refuse to be led astray by others, and they are armed with broad knowledge and a sharp intelligence with which to penetrate the essence of life and society. These are the qualities of a well-educated person.

- We should develop the wisdom to clearly and rationally discern the truth, but at the same time, even if the present outlook may appear hopeless, we must not despair. With the conviction that "I will definitely scale the summit of my ideals," and with firm belief in the great potential inherent in human beings, please continue your quest.

- Well-educated individuals do not remain locked in their own nation's culture; they study the cultures of the world and absorb what these cultures have to offer. This is the first requirement for being considered truly well-educated — in other words, to be capable of transcending one's own narrow world.

- One of the cornerstones of education lies in a mother's capacity to believe in her children, to support them and inspire in them a sense of confidence.

- Children in general are usually much more adult than their parents give them credit for being. They are capable of many things. Adults should not judge children according to their own arbitrary standards, telling them they can't do this or that because they are children. When we interact with children, we should always accord them due respect as unique individuals, allowing them to give free rein to their potential. Within each child exists a fine adult. It is important that we speak to that adult. This will lead to the development of the child's character.

- Value-creation is not something distant and removed from our lives. Any revolution or reform begins with the things closest or of most immediate concern to us. We must not run away from the problems that confront us in our daily lives, but rather take them on with courage. Value is created through such efforts, and from here waves of hope expand among people.

- President Makiguchi endeavored, by means of education and religious faith, to foster people who could create their own happiness, human beings who could create value. There is no other way to bring happiness to the human race. The concept of value creation (*soka*) formulated by Mr. Makiguchi focuses on the values of beauty, benefit and good. These are just alternative names for happiness. Although it is possible to inherit property, it is impossible to inherit happiness. We could replace the word *property* with *rank* or *knowledge* and the same would hold true.

Endnotes

Preface

1. Alfred Birnbaum, trans., Dayle M. Bethel, ed., *Education for Creative Living: Ideas and Proposals of Tsunesaburo Makiguchi* (Ames, IA: Iowa State University Press, 1989), 17.
2. *The Complete Writings of Ralph Waldo Emerson: Complete in One Volume* (New York: William H. Wise & Co., 1929), 990.
3. Dayle M. Bethel, *Makiguchi the Value Creator: Revolutionary Japanese Educator and Founder of the Soka Gakkai* (New York: Weatherhill, 1994), 154.

Introduction

1. John Dewey, *The School and Society* (Chicago: The University of Chicago Press, 1990), 18.
2. Tsunesaburo Makiguchi, *Makiguchi Tsunesaburo Zenshu* [The Complete Works of Tsunesaburo Makiguchi], vol. 1 (Tokyo: Daisan Bunmei-sha, 1983), 15.
3. Ibid., vol. 5 (Tokyo: Daisan Bunmei-sha, 1982), 27.
4. Ibid., vol. 2 (Tokyo: Daisan Bunmei-sha, 1981), 341.
5. Ibid., vol. 1, 15.
6. Ibid., vol. 10 (Tokyo: Daisan Bunmei-sha, 1987), 7.
7. Ibid., vol. 2, 399.
8. John Dewey, *The Collected Works of John Dewey, 1882–1953, The Middle Works: 1899–1925*, vol. 10, ed. Jo Ann Boydston (Carbondale: Southern Illinois University Press, 1969–1991), 204.
9. Tsunesaburo Makiguchi, *Zenshu*, vol. 5, 8.
10. Ibid., vol. 4 (Tokyo: Daisan Bunmei-sha, 1981), 27.

11. Ibid., vol. 5, 12.
12. Ibid., vol. 7 (Tokyo: Daisan Bunmei-sha, 1982), 183.
13. Ibid., vol. 6 (Tokyo: Daisan Bunmei-sha, 1983), 285. Tsunesaburo Makiguchi, *Education for Creative Living* (Ames, Iowa: Iowa State University Press, 1989), 168.
14. Ibid., vol. 6, 289.
15. Ibid., vol. 5, 20. Tsunesaburo Makiguchi, *Education for Creative Living*, 7–8.
16. Genichiro Isonokami, *Makiguchi Tsunesaburo to Nitobe Inazo* [Tsunesaburo Makiguchi and Nitobe Inazo] (Tokyo: Regulus Library, Daisan Bunmei-sha, Co., Ltd., 1993), 150.
17. Tsunesaburo Makiguchi, *Zenshu*, vol. 5, 236. Tsunesaburo Makiguchi, *Education for Creative Living*, 61.
18. John Dewey, *The Public and Its Problems* (Chicago: Gateway Books, 1946), 203.
19. John Dewey, *The School and Society*, 17.
20. Tsunesaburo Makiguchi, *Zenshu*, vol. 8 (Tokyo: Daisan Bunmei-sha, 1984), 388.
21. Ibid., vol. 6, 199. Tsunesaburo Makiguchi, *Education for Creative Living*, 153.
22. John Dewey, *The School and Society*, 14, 18.
23. Tsunesaburo Makiguchi, *Zenshu*, vol. 6, 209.
24. Ibid., vol. 6, 212.
25. John Dewey, *Freedom and Culture* (New York: Prometheus Books, 1989), 13.
26. Tsunesaburo Makiguchi, *Zenshu*, vol. 10 (Tokyo: Daisan Bunmei-sha, 1985), 6.
27. Takehisa Tsuji, ed. *Makiguchi Tsunesaburo Shingen-shu* [An Anthology of Tsunesaburo Makiguchi's Maxims] (Tokyo: Daisan Bunmei-sha, 1994), 26–27.
28. Tsunesaburo Makiguchi, *Zenshu*, vol. 10, 206. Japan. Special Higher Police, "Soka Kyoiku Gakkai Honbu Kankeisha no Chianijiho Ihan Jiken Kenkyo" [The Arrest of Persons Related with Soka Kyoiku Gakkai Headquarters for the Charge of Violating the Peace Preservation Law], *Tokko Geppo* [Monthly Report of the Special Higher Police] (July 1943), 127–28.

29. Tsunesaburo Makiguchi, *Zenshu*, vol. 10, 203. *Tokko Geppo*, 152, 156.
30. John Dewey, *A Common Faith* (New Haven: Yale University Press, 1934), 52.
31. Tsunesaburo Makiguchi, *Zenshu*, vol. 10, 146. *Tokko Geppo*, 146.
32. Nichiren, *The Writings of Nichiren Daishonin*, vol. 1 (Tokyo: Soka Gakkai, 2006), 1125.
33. Tsunesaburo Makiguchi, *Zenshu*, vol. 5, 232.
34. Ibid., vol. 8, 188. *Tokko Geppo*, 139–40.
35. Ibid., vol. 8, 63.
36. Ibid., vol. 10, 84.
37. Ibid., vol. 10, 26.
38. Ibid., vol. 8, 192. *Tokko Geppo*, 143–44.
39. Nichiren, *The Writings of Nichiren Daishonin*, vol. 1, 1121.

Chapter 1

1. The United Nations Conference on Environment and Development, also known as the Rio Summit or Earth Summit, was held in Rio de Janeiro, June 3–14, 1992. The 2002 World Summit on Sustainable Development, held in Johannesburg, South Africa, August 26–September 4, 2002, is sometimes referred to as Earth Summit 2002 or "Rio+10."
2. EarthKAM (Earth Knowledge Acquired by Middle School Students) is a NASA-sponsored program that enables middle school students to program a digital camera on board the International Space Station to photograph a variety of geographical targets for study in the classroom.
3. The Green Belt Movement is an indigenous grassroots, nongovernmental organization based in Nairobi, Kenya, and established by Wangari Maathai in 1977. The Green Belt Movement organized poor, rural women in Kenya to plant trees, combat deforestation, restore their main source of fuel for cooking, generate income and stop soil erosion. In 2004, Maathai received the Nobel Peace Prize for her efforts.

Chapter 2

1. Tsunesaburo Makiguchi, *Zenshu*, vol. 1, 8.
2. Simone Weil. "The Responsibility of Writers," *The Simone Weil Reader*, ed. George A. Panichas (Mt. Kisco, New York: Moyer Bell Limited, 1977), 288.
3. cf. Hitoshi Nagai and Yoshiyuki Koizumi, *Nazehito o koroshite wa naranaino ka?* (Why Is It Wrong To Kill People?) (Tokyo: Kawadeshoboshinsha, 1998).
4. Albert A. Likhanov, *Wakamonotachi no kokuhaku* [The Confessions of Youth], trans. Ayako Iwahara (Tokyo: Shindokushoshinsha, 1988), 161.
5. Norman Cousins, *Human Options* (New York: W. W. Norton & Company, 1981), 40.
6. Johan Galtung and Daisaku Ikeda, *Choose Peace: A Dialogue Between Johan Galtung and Daisaku Ikeda* (London: Pluto Press, 1995), 64.
7. Fyodor Dostoyevsky, *The House of the Dead*, trans. H. Sutherland Edwards (London: M. Dent & Sons, Ltd., 1962), 55–56.
8. Jean Jacques Rousseau, "Discourse on the Origin and Foundations of Inequality Among Men," *Rousseau's Political Writings*, ed. Alan Ritter and Julia Conaway Bondanella, trans. Julia Conaway Bondanella (New York: W. W. Norton & Company, 1988), 7.
9. *The Vimalakirti Sutra*, trans. Burton Watson from the Chinese version by Kumarajiva (New York: Columbia University Press, 1997), 65.
10. Mahatma Gandhi, *All Men Are Brothers: Autobiographical Reflections* (New York: The Continuum Publishing Co., 1990), 63.
11. Abraham H. Maslow, *Religions, Values, and Peak-Experiences* (New York: The Viking Press, 1970), 49.
12. Ibid., 50–52.
13. Shugoro Yamamoto, *Nagai saka* [The Long Slope] (Tokyo: Shinchosha, 1971), 17.
14. Albert Jacquard, *Petite philosophie à l'usage des non-philosophes* [A Modest Philosophy for Non-Philosophers] (n.p.: Calmann-Lévy, 1997), 18.

15. Leo Tolstoy, *Anna Karenina: A Novel in Eight Parts*, trans. Richard Pevear and Larissa Volokhonsky (New York: Viking-Penguin Putnam Inc., 2000), 792.
16. Ibid., 794.
17. Ibid., 795.
18. Ibid., 796.
19. Ibid., 809.
20. Ibid., 813–14.
21. Ibid., 815.

Chapter 3
1. *Chuo Koron*, September 1999 issue.
2. 1868–1912. Considered the beginning of Japan's modern period.
3. *Kyoiku Kihon Ho*. Promulgated on March 31, 1947.
4. Emperor Meiji, *Kyoiku Chokugo*, issued on October 30, 1890, it remained in effect until the end of World War II.
5. Kyushu–Okinawa Summit Meeting 2000 site, <http:Levywww.g8kyushuokinawa.go.jp/e/documents/it1.html>.
6. cf. José Ortega y Gasset, *The Revolt of the Masses* (New York: W. W. Norton & Company, Inc., 1932).
7. Tsunesaburo Makiguchi, *Zenshu*, vols. 1 and 2.
8. Nobukiyo Takahashi, *Mori ni asobu: Dorogame-san no sekai* (At Play in the Forest: The World of the Mud Turtle) (Tokyo: Asahi Shimbunsha, 1992).
9. Tsunesaburo Makiguchi, *Zenshu*, vols. 5 and 6.
10. *Buddhism in Action*, vol. 2 (Tokyo: NSIC, 1985), 342.
11. Tsunesaburo Makiguchi, *Zenshu*, vol. 9 (Tokyo: 1936, reprint, Daisanbunmei-sha, 1988).
12. Tsunesaburo Makiguchi, *Zenshu*, vol. 8.
13. The University of Chicago Laboratory Schools website, <http:Levywww.ucls.uchicago.edu/>.
14. "The Moral Equivalent of War," speech given at Stanford University, 1906.

Chapter 4

1. John Dewey, *The Public and Its Problems*, 154.
2. Henry David Thoreau, "The Village" in *Walden, The Selected Works of Thoreau*, ed. Walter Harding, Cambridge ed. (Boston: Houghton Mifflin Company, 1975), 359.
3. Alex Wayman and Hideko Wayman, trans., *The Lion's Roar of Queen Srimala: A Buddhist Scripture on the Tathagata-garbha Theory* (New York: Columbia University Press, 1974), 65.
4. Nichiren, "Opening of the Eyes," *Selected Writings of Nichiren*, ed. Philip B. Yampolsky, trans. Burton Watson, et al. (New York: Columbia University Press, 1990), 56.
5. Takehisa Tsuji, ed., *An Anthology of Tsunesaburo Makiguchi's Works* (Japanese) (Tokyo: Daisan Bunmei-sha, 1994), 40.
6. John Dewey, *The Public and Its Problems*, 213.
7. Tsunesaburo Makiguchi, *Zenshu*, vol. 7, 183.
8. Tsunesaburo Makiguchi, *Zenshu*, vol. 6, 289.
9. Charter of the United Nations, Article I.
10. Tsunesaburo Makiguchi, *Zenshu*, vol. 8, 365.

Chapter 5

1. Tsunesaburo Makiguchi, *Zenshu*, vol. 9, 97, and vol. 6, 71, 180.
2. Ibid., vol. 4, 27.
3. Ibid., vol. 5, 16.
4. Ibid., vol. 5, 232.
5. Ibid., vol. 10, 84.
6. Takehisa Tsuji, *Anthology*, 26–27.
7. The Peace Preservation Act of 1925 was one of the prime legal tools used to suppress all forms of dissident expression. The Religious Organizations Act of 1940 consolidated all religious organizations in Japan under Shinto leadership.
8. Josei Toda, *Collected Works of Josei Toda*, vol. 8 (in Japanese) (Tokyo: Seikyo Shimbunsha, 1988), 463.
9. Tsunesaburo Makiguchi, *Zenshu*, vol. 10, 209–10.
10. Nichiren, *The Writings of Nichiren Daishonin*, vol. 2 (Tokyo: Soka Gakkai, 2006), 1060.
11. Tsunesaburo Makiguchi, *Zenshu*, vol. 10, 85, 276–78.
12. Ibid., vol. 6, 69.

Chapter 6
1. Also known as the Mukden Incident or the September 18 Incident. On September 18, 1931, near Mukden (now Shenyang) in southern Manchuria, a section of railroad owned by Japan's South Manchuria Railway was dynamited. Blaming Chinese dissidents, the Imperial Japanese Army invaded Manchuria, leading to the establishment of Manchukuo the following year. It is still unclear who perpetrated this sabotage, but the prevailing view is that Japanese militarists staged the explosion to provide a pretext for war.

Chapter 9
1. Mr. Makiguchi argued that the highest object of life is happiness and that the goal of life is nothing but the attainment and creation of value, which is in itself happiness. He said that education is the means whereby individuals can acquire competence as creators of value and thereby find happiness in the process.

Chapter 10
1. John Silber, *Straight Shooting: What's Wrong with America and How to Fix It* (New York: Harper & Row, 1989), 304.
2. Jean Jacques Rousseau, *Émile*, trans. Barbara Foxley M. A. (London: J. M. Dent & Sons Ltd., 1948 reprint), 51.
3. Xenophon, "Memorabilia," vol. 4 of *Xenophon*, trans. E. C. Marchant (London: William Heinemann Ltd. and Cambridge, Massachusetts: Harvard University Press, 1923), 95.
4. Ibid., 99.
5. Masahiko Fujiwara, "Nihonjin no Hinkaku" (Japanese Refinement), *Gakushi Geppo*, (March 1993), 61.
6. Plato, "Protagoras," vol. 4 of *Plato*, trans. W. R. M. Lamb, M.A. (London: William Heinemann Ltd., and Cambridge, Massachusetts: Harvard University Press, 1924), 257.
7. Ibid., 371.
8. Ibid., 299.
9. *The Essays of Michel de Montaigne*, vol. 1, ed. and trans. Jacob Zeitlin (New York: Alfred A. Knopf, Inc., 1934), 137.

Included Works

Introduction: John Dewey and Tsunesaburo Makiguchi: Confluences of Thought and Action (June 2001)
 Reprinted with the permission of the Center for Dewey Studies. Previously published as the inaugural paper in the series "Occasional Papers" (Carbondale: Center for Dewey Studies, Southern Illinois University, June 2001) at http://www.siuc.edu/~deweyctr/scholarship_papers.html.

Chapter 1: The Challenge of Global Empowerment: Education for a Sustainable Future (August 26–September 4, 2002)
 Presented on the occasion of the 2002 World Summit on Sustainable Development.

Chapter 2: Reviving Education (January 9, 2001)
 Previously published as "Reviving Education: The Brilliance of the Inner Spirit," *Living Buddhism*, July 2001 (Santa Monica, Calif.: SGI-USA), 22–36.

Chapter 3: Serving the Essential Needs of Education (September 29, 2001)
 Previously published as "Building a Society Serving the Essential Needs of Education," *Living Buddhism*, February 2001 (Santa Monica, Calif.: SGI-USA), 10–27.

Chapter 4: Education Toward Global Citizenship (June 13, 1996)
 Previously published as "Lecture: Thoughts on Education for Global Citizenship," *SGI President Daisaku Ikeda's Addresses in the United States* (Santa Monica, Calif.: SGI-USA, 1996), 59–75.

Chapter 5: An Outspoken Advocate of Educational Reform (June 4, 1996)
   Previously published as "Lecture: Makiguchi's Lifelong Pursuit of Justice and Humane Values," *SGI President Daisaku Ikeda's Addresses in the United States* (Santa Monica, Calif.: SGI-USA, 1996), 16–34.

Chapter 6: Teachers of My Childhood (2004)
   Previously published in President Daisaku Ikeda's book *One by One* (Sonoma, Calif.: Dunhill Publishing, 2004).

Chapter 7: The Teacher's Art (1998)
   First published as part of an essay series in the Philippine magazine *Mirror* in 1998.

Chapter 8: An Unforgettable Teacher (1998)
   First published as part of an essay series in the Philippine magazine *Mirror* in 1998.

Chapter 9: Humanity in Education (August 24, 1984)
   Previously published as "Thoughts on the Aims of Education," *Buddhism in Action*, vol. 2 (Tokyo: NSIC, 1985), 328.

Chapter 10: Perspective on Virtue (January 26, 1992)
   Previously published as "A Renaissance of Hope and Harmony," *Seikyo Times*, April 1992 (Santa Monica, Calif.: SGI-USA), 6–23.

Chapter 11: A True Restoration of Humanity (April 9, 1973)
   Previously published as "On Being Creative," *A Lasting Peace, Collected Addresses of Daisaku Ikeda* (New York: John Weatherhill, Inc., 1981), 48–58.

Chapter 12: The Fight To Live a Creative Life (April 18, 1974)
   Previously published as "Creative Lives," *A Lasting Peace, Collected Addresses of Daisaku Ikeda* (New York: John Weatherhill, Inc., 1981) 126–34.

Index

A
academic ability, improving, 78
activities, of the SGI, 46
admissions policies, reforming university, 101–02
air raid, of Tokyo, 144–45
Akademeia, 194–98
Aliso Viejo, 103
American universities, high standards of, 105–06
Anan, Kofi, 37
ancient seats of learning, based on humanism, 194–97
Anna Karenina (Tolstoy), 68–71
authority, anger at, 132; demonic nature of, 2; the private university as a stronghold against, 205. *See also* educational authorities

B
balanced reform, 94–96
Bethel, Dayle M., xiii
Bodhisattva Way, 59
books, like good friends, 65–66
Boston Research Center for the 21st Century, 84
Buddhism, 30–31, 45, 55, 113–14, 126. *See also* Mahayana Buddhism; Nichiren Buddhism
Bushido (Nitobe), 172, 183

C
causality, universal law of, 29–31
Center for Dewey Studies, 1
Center for Excellence in Teaching and Learning, 103
character, building through reading, 64–66
children, as central to theory and practice of education, 9; as the mirror of society, 79–80, 177; more grown up than they're considered, 222; quickly detecting apathy and cynicism, 54; toward a century radiant with the smiles, 107–08
China, 143
civilization, having reached a turning point, 201; university as a basic current of, 193–94
collective life, engaging consciously in, 7
Columbia University, 20; 84; Teacher's College, xiv, 20, 109
competition, humanitarian, 6–8
compulsory religious education, in Japan, 61–63
concern and compassion, 45
confidence, 136
connections, reading literature as an opportunity to make, 167
Constitution. *See* Japanese Constitution
contributive, way of life, 45–46
Cousins, Norman, 53–54
creativity, the badge of humanity, 168–71; defining, 209; and experimentation, 96–99; life's natural tendency to, 209; and living creatively, 66, 203–10
crime, juvenile, in Japan, 76; Russian view of, 57–59
crisis, education in, 75–77
curricula. *See* educational curricula

D
Darwinian image of evolution, Makiguchi and Dewey influenced by, 6

death, message of cherry trees in the midst of, 145
Deductive Guide to Arithmetic (Toda), 99
depth psychology, 164
Desana, of the Amazon, 44–45
Devadatta, 55
developmental education, 120
devotion, pride and, 199–201
Dewey, John, 4, 32, 109, 125; influenced by Darwinian image of evolution, 6; Laboratory School of, 19, 99; pragmatism of, 17
dialogue, education based on, 213; and engagement, 45–46; genuine reality revealed through, 56; of Shakyamuni, 196
divisiveness, pathology of, 115
Dostoevsky, Fyodor, 57–59, 71
drug abuse, worldwide problem of, 76
Dunhuang, 140

E
Earth Charter, 41; SGI and, 42
Earth Summit, 35, 38
education, 137; based on dialogue, 213; Buddhist perspective of, vii; children as central to theory and practice, 9, 143; in crisis, 75–77; debasement of, 151; foundation of, 139; and the future, 72–74; history of Japanese, 207; humanistic, vi, 47, 117; humanity in, 161–75; independence of, 91–94; integrating into the life of society, 18, 79, 217; Japanese nationalist agenda for, 9, 156–57, 162–63; moral of Heracles, 181–82; power of, 143; purpose of, v, 150–51, 213; reclaiming the ancient vision of, vii–ix; recommendations for, 96–108, 214–16; redefining, 13, 163; restoring humanity to, 162–64; reviving, 49–74; serving the essential needs of, 75–108; for sustainable development, 35–45; toward global citizenship, 109–21; for winning over one's own weakness, 116
The Education as Transformation Project, viii, 60
Education as Transformation award, viii
educational authorities, Makiguchi's confrontations with, 12–13
Educational Counseling Program, 72–74
educational curricula, to cultivate zest for living, 78; at Soka University of America, 103–04; world literature in, 65
educational ideals, Makiguchi's, xi
educational reform, superficial attempts at, 92
educators, enriching the work of, vi–vii
Ego, versus Self, 55
egoism, struggle to rise above, 116
elementary education, 147
Eliot, T.S., 173
Emerson, Ralph Waldo, xi
empathy, 39
emperor, views of Makiguchi on, 24–25
empirical method, 14, 26
empowerment, 46
An Encouragement of Learning (Fukuzawa), 166
English education, promoting in elementary schools, 106

Index

enrichment, through reading, 71–72
environmental education, 38–39, 41–43, 120; in school curriculum, 40
environmental ethics, 43–44
Essays (Montaigne), 186
evil, aversion to, 52–55
evolution, influence of Darwinian image of, 6
exhibitions, SGI organized, 40–41
experiential learning, for global citizenship, 17–21
experimentalism, creativity and, 17, 96–99

F

Faust (Goethe), 165
fighting, to live a creative life, 203–10
fostering, the future, 138–39
freedom, increased spiritual, 197–99; indiscriminant advocacy of, 95; of thought, 205
Freedom and Culture (Dewey), 21
Friedmann, Georges, 206
Fröbel, Friedrich Wilhelm August, 14
Fujiwara, Masahiko, 183
Fukuzawa, Yukichi, 165–66
Fundamental Law of Education, 62–63, 80–83, 86, 162
future, education and the, 72–74

G

Galtung, Johan, 56
Gandhi, Mahatma, 59
G8 Education Summit, 94
The Geography of Human Life (Makiguchi), 4–8, 89, 116, 125, 215
global citizenship, education toward, 109–21; experiential learning for, 17–21; Makiguchi promoting idea of, 5
global environment, protecting, 35–38
Goethe, Johann Wolfgang von, 71, 165
good, aversion to, 52–55
goodness, defining, 115
Gorbachev, Mikhail, 42
Gorgias, 181
grassroots movements, 40–43
Great T'ang Record of Western Countries, 194
"greater self," 46
Green Belt Movement, 42–43
Green Cross International, 42
Gress, Esther, 47–48
growth, watching over, 138–39

H

happiness, xii, 28, 45, 87–88, 112, 114, 133, 150–51, 153, 223; society confuses pleasure with, 86–88
Harvard University, 56
Henderson, Hazel, 44
Heracles, moral education of, 181–82; 184
heritage. *See* philosophical heritage
Hippias, 181
The House of the Dead (Dostoevsky), 57–59
Hsuan Tsang, 194
Hugo, Victor, 163
human beings, 150
human bonds, depending on, 90–91; restoring, 89–91
human happiness, seeking together, 7, 46
human life, geography of, 4–6
human potential, tragic waste of, 11

human revolution, 47
human rights education, 120
humanism, ancient seats of learning based on, 194–97; Buddhist, 2
humanistic education, 47, 74, 87, 102, 117, 129; for raising humanistic people, 213
humanitarian competition, 6–8
humanity, capacity for language, 56; creativity as the badge of, 168–71; in education, 161–75; restoring to education, 162–64; true restoration of, 189–202; uniting, 44
Huyghe, René, 208

I
Ikeda Center for Peace, Learning, and Dialogue. *See* Boston Research Center for the 21st Century
Imperial Rescript on Education, 82–83, 87
imperialism, Makiguchi on, 5
independence, of education, 91–94
individual, sacred and inviolable rights of, 5; and world, viii
Indra, palace of, 113
Information and Communication Technology (IT), 85–86
inner realm of the soul, and religious sentiment, 57–59
intellectual heritage, university as a repository of, 193
interconnectedness, 39, 44–47
International Decade for a Culture of Peace and Nonviolence for the Children of the World, 107
international exchange, promoting, 105–07
international outlook, 171–75

International Year of Volunteers, 101
Iroquois, of North America, 45
island nations, special role for, 8
IT. *See* Information and Communication Technology

J
Jacquard, Albert, 67–68
James, William, 100
Japan, compulsory religious education in, 61–62; increasing social pathology in, 88; history of, 136–37; Ministry of Education, 75, 98
Japanese Constitution, 61, 162
Jasienski, Bruno, 53
Jesus of Nazareth, 59
Jinsei Chirigaku (The Geography of Human Life) (Makiguchi), 4
Jishu Gakkan, 99
Jung, Carl, 55

K
Kachi Sozo (Value Creation), 22–23, 30, 128
Kaneko, Kentaro, 172
Kant, Immanuel, 84
Kawai, Hayao, 71
Kazanjian, Victor, 60–61
Kenyan Green Belt Movement, 42
kindness, teacher's, 141–42
King, Martin Luther King, Jr., 59
Kissinger, Henry, 172
knowledge, 151; absorbing fully, 221
ko-yarai, 170
Kubota, Masataka, 15

L
language, humanity's capacity for, 56

League of Nations, 136
learning, flight from, 77–78
Levine, Arthur, 111
liberal arts education, 104
life, and happiness, 28, 88; and creativity, 209; sanctity of, 133
life-to-life communication, xiii
Likhanov, Albert A., 53
literature, an opportunity to make connections, 167; in educational curriculum, 65
local community, Makiguchi's view of, 43
Lotus Sutra, 27

M

Mahayana Buddhism, 59, 194
Makiguchi, Tsunesaburo, vii–viii, xiv, 46, 109–12, 123–33; arrested by the Special Higher Police, 24, 129–32, 158; charges against, 158; childhood trials of, 2–3, 155; confluences of thought and action, 1–32; confrontation with educational authorities, 12–13, 157–58; courage displayed by, 158; death of, 131–32, 158; education theory of, 156–57; importance of human beings for, 159; influence of the ideas of, 158–59; influenced by Darwinian image of evolution, 6; outspoken advocate of educational reform, 91–94, 109–12, 123–33; as a school principal, 156; targeted as a thought criminal, 24; teaching career and educational philosophy, xi–xiv, 8–11, 87, 156
Makiguchi, The Value Creator (Bethel), xiii
Manchurian Incident, 136

Maslow, Abraham H., 59–60
Meiji Constitution of 1889, 5
Meiji era, 80; early years in, 2–4
Meno, 184
Middle Ages, 190–91, 198
military fascism, 128–29
Ministry of Education, survey by, 50
modern education, xi
Montaigne, Michel de, 186
moral equivalent of war, 100
Mori, Ogai, 174
Morito, Tatsuo, 82

N

Nagai saka (The Long Slope) (Yamamoto), 65
Nalanda, 193–94, 198
National Council on Educational Reform (NCER), 81–82, 91–92, 98
National Institute for Educational Research of Japan, 93
National Mobilization Law of 1938, 22, 157
nationalism, in Japan, 143; narrow minded, Makiguchi on, 5
Nazi, 151
NCER. *See* National Council on Educational Reform
needs of education, serving essential, 75–108
neo-renaissance, need for, 201
Nichiren Buddhism, xii, 16, 22; history of, 25–28; Makiguchi's studies of, 26–29
Nitobe, Inazo, 172, 183

O

Okinawa Charter on Global Information Society, 85
Okinawa-Kyushu Summit, 85

Okri, Ben, 48
Olympics, 137
opening the door, 209–10
Ortega y Gasset, José, 87
other, self in absence of the, 55–57

P
Palmer, Parker, v
paradigm shift, 83–86
peace education, 120
Peace Preservation Act of 1925, 30, 129 158; 1941 revision of, 22
peace and prosperity, humanity's, xiv
Peccei, Aurelio, 46–47
Pedagogy of Value-Creating Education, The (Makiguchi), 46
Péguy, Charles Pierre, 210
people, "roots" for, 138
philosophical heritage, need for a profound, 192–93
philosophy, of value creation, 15–17
physical strength, 137, 142
Plato, 169, 181, 184, 194, 198
pleasure, a society that confused happiness with, 86–88
positivism, 14
power, and wisdom, 206–09; of youth, 213
Power and the Wisdom, The (Friedmann), 206
pragmatism, philosophy of, 17
praise, 136, 152
pride, and devotion, 199–201
private universities, 198, 200; special nature of, 204–06; as stronghold against governmental authority, 205
Prodicus, 181, 184
profiting ourselves, while profiting others, 7
Protagoras, 181, 184

R
A Quiet Revolution, 36; Soka Gakkai International supporting, 37
reading, building character through, 64–66; enrichment through, 71–72
reality, revealed through genuine dialogue, 56
reform, balanced, 94–96; of universities, fundamental, 101–02
religion, view on, 25–29, 187
Religious Organizations Law of 1932, 22
religious sentiment, cultivation of, 63–64; inner realm of the soul and, 57–59
Remengesau, Tommy E, Jr., on global warming, 36
Renaissance, 190–91, 194, 196
restoration, of humanity, true, 189–202; new, 201–02
reverence for life, 44–46
rights of the individual, sacred and inviolable, 5
Rousseau, Jean Jacques, 58, 179, 182

S
sakuramori, 138
sanctity of life, 108, 110, 127, 133
scholarships, 106
School and Society, The (Dewey), 4, 9
school systems, in Japan, 150
schools, as an embryonic society, 18; governmental, 205; suicides in, 76
secret police, Makiguchi under surveillance by, 23–24, 128–29, 158
Seikyo Shimbun, 52

self, in absence of the other, 55–57; ego *versus*, 55
self-knowledge, 208

SGI-USA, Victory Over Violence movement in, 107
Shakyamuni, 30, 55; dialogues of, 196–97; Thurman's understanding of, 84
Shoin, Yoshida, 89
Silber, John, 178–80, 182
Simon Wiesenthal Center, 123
smiles of children, toward a century radiant with, 107–08
socialism, collapse of in Eastern Europe, 177–78
society, children as the mirror of, 79–80, 177; confuses happiness with pleasure, 86–88; integrating education into the life of, 18, 74, 217
Socrates, 14, 88, 170–71, 181, 184, 195, 208
"soka," origin of, 16
Soka educational system, xiii
Soka Gakkai (Value Creation Society), 155
Soka Gakkai educators' society, 158
Soka Gakkai International, viii, 186
Soka Kyoiku Gakkai, 1–2, 17, 22–24, 28, 30, 127–28; first meeting of, 127; guiding principles of published, 22; Makiguchi's view of, 28
Soka kyoikugaku taikei. See System of Value-Creating Pedagogy, The
Soka school system, 158–59
Soka University of America, xiv; Center for Excellence in Teaching and Learning, 103; contributions of, 102–05; Entrance Ceremony of, 189, 203; exists for its students, 219; humanistic approach to education, 61; objectives for, 197–98
Sophists, 181, 184, 194
soul, inner realm of, 57–59
Special Higher Police, Makiguchi and Toda arrested by, 24
spiritual freedom, increased, 197–98
spiritual transformation, Tolstoy's portrait of, 68–71
spirituality, regaining, 70
Srimala, vow of, 114–15
Stevenson, Robert Louis, 54
Strong, Maurice, 41
students, Soka University of America existing for, 218; teachers' influence on, 219
study, 150
Suematsu, Kentaro, 172
System of Value-Creating Pedagogy, The (Makiguchi), 9–12, 51, 92, 99, 109, 127, 132, 159, 216

T
Takahashi, Nobukiyo, 90
Tanaka, Chigaku, 27
teachers, influence on students, 136–40, 142, 146–49, 151–53, 156, 220; reassessing role of, 13–15
teaching, 147
theorists, 147
Thessaloniki Declaration of the International Conference on Environment and Society, 38, 41
Thoreau, Henry David, 113
Thurman, Robert, 84
Toda, Josei, viii, xii, 1, 16, 31, 62, 66, 93, 110, 118, 127, 132, 151,

158, 218–19; arrested by the Special Higher Police, 24, 158; Yamashita's view of, xiii
Tokko Geppo, 24–25
Tolstoy, Leo, portrait of spiritual transformation, 68–71
totalitarianism, in the shadow of, 21–25
Toynbee, Arnold J., 199
transformation, Tolstoy's portrait of spiritual, 68–71
truth, wisdom to discern, 222

U

U.N. International Decade for a Culture of Peace and Nonviolence for the Children of the World, 107
U.N. International Year of Volunteers, 101
UNESCO, 38, 107
United Nations, understanding the potential of, 119
universal law of causality, 29–31
universities, as a basic current of civilization, 193–94; emergence in the West, 190–91; fundamental reform of, 101–02; origin of, 191; reforming admission policies, 101–02; special nature of private, 204–06

V

value creation, philosophy of, viii, 15–17, 112, 127, 156–57, 215, 223
values, absence of, 59–61
Victory Over Violence (VOV) movement, 107
Vimalakirti bodhisattva, 59
Vinci, Leonardo da, 192
virtual reality, dangers of, 67–68
virtue, perspectives on, 177–87
volunteer activities, 99–101
VOV. *See* Victory Over Violence movement

W

Wannsee Conference, 151
Weil, Simone, 52
Wellesley College, v, 60
West, emergence of the university in the, 190–91
Whitehead, Alfred North, 168
Windelband, Wilhelm, 26
wisdom, 151; to discern truth, 222; ignored, 165; power and, 206–09; totality of, 164–68
world literature, in the educational curriculum, 65
world peace, 137
World Summit of Educators, 40
WSSD (World Summit on Sustainable Development), 36–37, 47

X

Xenophon, 181

Y

Yamada, Taichi, 79–80
Yamamoto, Shugoro, 65
Yamashita, Hajime, xiii
Yoshikawa, Eiji, 139
youth, power of, 213